DEADLY DISEASES AND EPIDEMICS

HIV/AIDS

DEADLY DISEASES AND EPIDEMICS

HIV/AIDS

Patrick G. Guilfoile, Ph.D.

Consulting Editor
Hilary Babcock, M.D., M.P.H.,
Infectious Diseases Division,
Washington University School of Medicine,
Medical Director of Occupational Health (Infectious Diseases),
Barnes–Jewish Hospital and St. Louis Children's Hospital

Foreword by
David L. Heymann
World Health Organization

CHELSEA HOUSE
An Infobase Learning Company

HIV/AIDS

Chelsea House
An imprint of Infobase Learning
132 West 31st Street
New York NY 10001

Library of Congress Cataloging-in-Publication Data

Guilfoile, Patrick.
 HIV/AIDS / Patrick G. Guilfoile ; consulting editor, Hilary Babcock ; foreword by David Heymann.
     p. cm. — (Deadly diseases and epidemics)
  Rev. ed. of: HIV/AIDS / Consuelo M. Beck-Sague, Caridad Beck. ©2004.
  Includes bibliographical references and index.
  ISBN-13: 978-1-60413-465-0 (hardcover : alk. paper)
  ISBN-10: 1-60413-465-8 (hardcover : alk. paper)   1. AIDS (Disease)
I. Babcock, Hilary.   II. Beck-Sague, Consuelo M., 1952– HIV/AIDS.
III. Title.
  RC606.6.B43 2011
  616.97'92—dc22

                                                           2011012184

Text design by Terry Mallon
Cover design by Takeshi Takahashi
Composition by Newgen North America
Cover printed by Yurchak Publishing, Landisville, Pa.
Book printed and bound by Yurchak Publishing, Landisville, Pa.
Date printed: June 2011
Printed in the United States of America

This book is printed on acid-free paper.
All links and Web addresses were checked and verified to be correct at the time of publication. Because of the dynamic nature of the Web, some addresses and links may have changed since publication and may no longer be valid.

Table of Contents

Acknowledgments

I thank my wife, Audrey, for her support and assistance, and my father, Thomas, for his advice and expert proofreading skills.

Foreword

Communicable diseases kill and cause long-term disability. The microbial agents that cause them are dynamic, changeable, and resilient: They are responsible for more than 14 million deaths each year mainly in developing countries.

Approximately 46% of all deaths in the developing world are due to communicable diseases, and almost 90% of these deaths are from AIDS, tuberculosis, malaria, and acute diarrheal and respiratory infections of children. In addition to causing great human suffering these high-mortality communicable diseases have become major obstacles to economic development. They are a challenge to control either because of the lack of effective vaccines, or because the drugs that are used to treat them are becoming less effective because of antimicrobial drug resistance.

Millions of people, especially those who are poor and living in developing countries, are also at risk from disabling communicable diseases such as polio, leprosy, lymphatic filariasis, and onchocerciasis. In addition to human suffering and permanent disability, these communicable diseases create an economic burden—both on the workforce that handicapped persons are unable to join, and on their families and society, upon which they must often depend for economic support.

Finally, the entire world is at risk of the unexpected communicable diseases, those that are called emerging or reemerging infections. Infection is often unpredictable because risk factors for transmission are not understood, or because it often results from organisms that cross the species barrier from animals to humans. The cause is often viral, such as Ebola and Marburg hemorrhagic fevers and severe acute respiratory syndrome (SARS). In addition to causing human suffering and death, these infections place health workers at great risk and are costly to economies. Infections such as Bovine Spongiform Encephalopathy (BSE) and the associated new human variant of Creutzfeldt-Jakob disease (vCJD) in Europe, and avian influenza A (H5N1) in Asia, are reminders of the seriousness of emerging and reemerging infections. In addition, many of these infections have the potential to cause pandemics, which are a constant threat to our economies and public health security.

Science has given us vaccines and anti-infective drugs that have helped keep infectious diseases under control. Nothing demonstrates the effectiveness of vaccines better than the successful eradication of smallpox, the decrease in polio as the eradication program continues, and the decrease in measles when routine immunization programs are supplemented by mass vaccination campaigns.

Likewise, the effectiveness of anti-infective drugs is clearly demonstrated through prolonged life or better health in those infected with viral diseases such as AIDS, parasitic infections such as malaria, and bacterial infections such as tuberculosis and pneumococcal pneumonia.

But current research and development is not filling the pipeline for new anti-infective drugs as rapidly as resistance is developing, nor is vaccine development providing vaccines for some of the most common and lethal communicable diseases. At the same time, providing people with access to existing anti-infective drugs, vaccines, and goods such as condoms or bed nets—necessary for the control of communicable diseases in many developing countries—remains a great challenge.

Education, experimentation, and the discoveries that grow from them are the tools needed to combat high-mortality infectious diseases, diseases that cause disability, or emerging and reemerging infectious diseases. At the same time, partnerships between developing and industrialized countries can overcome many of the challenges of access to goods and technologies. This book may inspire its readers to set out on the path of drug and vaccine development, or on the path to discovering better public health technologies by applying our current understanding of the human genome and those of various infectious agents. Readers may likewise be inspired to help ensure wider access to those protective goods and technologies. Such inspiration, with pragmatic action, will keep us on the winning side of the struggle against communicable diseases.

David L. Heymann
Assistant Director General
Health Security and Environment
Representative of the Director General for Polio Eradication
World Health Organization
Geneva, Switzerland

1

What Are HIV and AIDS?

Ryan White was diagnosed with acquired immunodeficiency syndrome **(AIDS)** *in 1984 at the age of 13, after he became ill with a severe and unusual case of pneumonia. Ryan had a genetic condition called* **hemophilia,** *which resulted in poor blood clotting. To treat his hemophilia, he received a clotting factor made from the blood pooled from many donors. Some of this blood was infected with the human immunodeficiency virus* **(HIV),** *and he became infected. Once Ryan recovered from his bout with pneumonia, he tried to return to school. The local school district barred him from attending, out of a misinformed fear that he might infect other people. The case went to court, and Ryan was eventually allowed to attend school, but reaction by some in the community continued to be negative, and he eventually moved to another city and attended a different school. Ryan died at the age of 18, shortly before his high school graduation. Ryan's AIDS diagnosis occurred early in the epidemic, at about the same time HIV was identified. During that period, there was a great deal of public misunderstanding about HIV and AIDS. Ryan's case drew national attention, helped educate the public about HIV transmission, and reduced the stigma associated with the disease.*[1]

Ryan White was one of over 25 million people who have died from AIDS since the disease was first recognized in 1981. HIV likely claimed its first victims in Africa, perhaps in the 1930s, and probably reached the United States around 1970. The United Nations estimates that 34 million people are currently infected with HIV and 2.7 million new infections and about 2 million deaths from AIDS occur each year. In Africa alone, 15 million children are AIDS orphans and only half the people in Africa in need of treatment are receiving it. In three decades, AIDS has gone from being unknown to being the fourth leading cause of death worldwide.[2]

THE ORIGIN OF THE VIRUS

Many pathogens got their start infecting other animals before they crossed the species gap to humans. HIV is an example of just such a pathogen. The virus we now call HIV likely originated in chimpanzees in Cameroon in west-central Africa.[3] The chimpanzee virus, called SIV_{cpz} (simian immunodeficiency virus–chimpanzee), is an amalgamation of two other **SIV** viruses from red-capped mangabeys and greater spot-nosed monkeys. The current hypothesis is that chimpanzees simultaneously became infected with these two SIVs, leading to the development of SIV_{cpz}.[4] This may have happened when chimpanzees ate SIV-infected red-capped mangabeys and greater spot-nosed monkeys. The viruses then combined in the dually infected chimpanzees, and produced a hybrid virus that was now capable of infecting both chimpanzees and humans.[5] This virus establishes an infection but does not cause a noticeable disease in chimpanzees. However, the hybrid chimpanzee virus was apparently able to grow in human cells, and mutate to the point where it was able to cause disease in humans. How did the virus make the leap from chimpanzees to humans? The leading hypothesis is that transmission occurred when hunters butchered chimpanzees while preparing the meat for eating or for sale. During the butchering process, it was likely that blood from a chimpanzee got into the hunter's cut or wound, leading to an infection. The evidence supporting this idea comes primarily from a comparison of **DNA sequences** from chimpanzee viruses and HIV. Based on sequence comparisons, it appears that chimpanzee SIV has been transmitted to humans at least three times, although only one of these transmitted strains caused widespread infection.[6] It is sobering to realize that the HIV epidemic might never have happened if humans did not kill and eat chimpanzees.

DESCRIPTION OF HIV

Like almost all viruses, HIV is visible only with an electron microscope. The virus has a diameter of about 100 nm, which

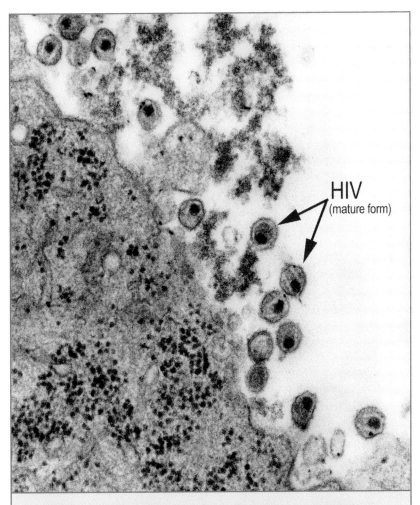

HIV
(mature form)

Figure 1.1 A transmission electron micrograph of mature HIV from a tissue sample. (Centers for Disease Control and Prevention)

is about 1/4000th the diameter of a human hair. As with other viruses, HIV can only reproduce inside cells. HIV primarily infects cells that are part of the human **immune system**, although HIV can infect many other types of cells as well. In particular, HIV primarily targets **CD4+ T-cells, macrophages,** and **dendritic cells**. CD4+ T-cells are a type of white blood cell that acts as a master regulator of the immune system, providing chemical signals that coordinate immune responses. Macrophages are white blood cells whose name literally means "large eaters." These cells seek out foreign matter, and then engulf and usually destroy the offending material. Dendritic cells have a similar origin and function to macrophages, but tend to be found in different tissues, such as the skin.

The interior of HIV contains the **genome** of the virus: two single-stranded **ribonucleic acid (RNA)** molecules that are 9,749 nucleotides in length. (A genome is the entire set of genetic instructions in an organism or a virus. RNA is a type of genetic material found in some viruses.) Several proteins are tethered to the RNA, inside the viral particle. These proteins include the **enzyme** reverse transcriptase, which is critical for replication of the virus, and integrase, which allows the virus to insert its genetic information into the genome of its host. (**DNA**, or deoxyribonucleic acid, is the genetic material found in the cells of all organisms.)

The viral RNA is enclosed in a structure called the **nucleocapsid**, a protein-containing capsule that helps prevent the RNA from being degraded when it enters a cell. Like other related viruses, the nucleocapsid in HIV is composed of a protein called p24. The nucleocapsid is surrounded by a structure called the envelope. The outer layer of the virus is primarily composed of a cell membrane that was pinched off an infected cell as HIV budded. This layer is decorated with HIV proteins, particularly the envelope proteins gp120 and gp41. These proteins play a critical role in HIV entry into host cells.

HIV is a **retrovirus**. As noted above, retroviruses have a genome composed of RNA, and this RNA is converted to DNA during the viral life cycle. The name *retrovirus* is based on the idea that, normally, information flow in biology is from DNA to RNA; retroviruses do it backward, converting information in RNA to DNA.

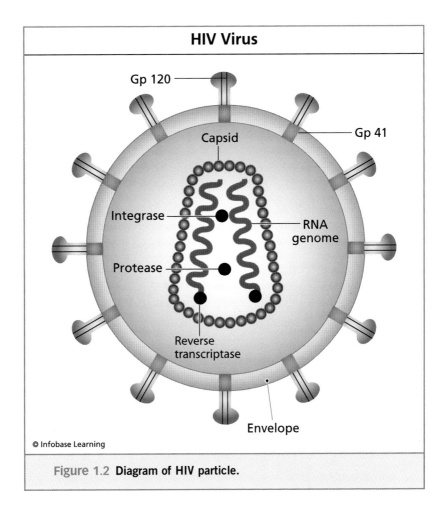

HIV Virus

Gp 120

Gp 41

Capsid

Integrase

RNA genome

Protease

Reverse transcriptase

Envelope

© Infobase Learning

Figure 1.2 **Diagram of HIV particle.**

COURSE OF HIV INFECTION AND SYMPTOMS OF HIV INFECTION

AIDS is caused by HIV. The symptoms of AIDS, and the timing of onset of AIDS, can vary greatly with different individuals, and in different countries. AIDS often develops within a few months when infants are infected at birth. In contrast, some adults may not develop symptoms for decades after contracting the virus. On average, though, adults will develop AIDS within 10 years following infection, if they are untreated.[7] Advanced treatment methods can make HIV undetectable in the blood, which greatly slows the progression to AIDS, or may stop it completely.

Following HIV infection, there is an incubation period that generally lasts from two weeks to a month. During this period, there are no overt symptoms of disease, although the virus is spreading throughout the body. The acute stage of HIV infection eventually presents as a nonspecific illness with flu-like symptoms, including fever, swollen lymph nodes, muscle aches, and related signs. This stage typically lasts about a month. Following the acute stage, which usually ends by six weeks to two months after the initial infection, there is no outward sign of disease. The virus continues to infect cells and replicate, but the immune system is still reasonably intact. This stage can last from months to decades. The final phase in HIV infection is the progression to AIDS. Prior to the availability of effective treatments, death usually followed within one to two years of an AIDS diagnosis. With effective treatment, the life span of AIDS patients has expanded substantially.

The hallmark of AIDS is frequent, severe infections, often caused by innocuous microbes that do not infect people with a normally functioning immune system. These infections lead to a variety of symptoms such as pneumonia (often caused by *Pneumocystis*), a yeast infection of the mouth known as thrush, and changes in the skin, often red or purple patches (which may be caused by a type of cancer called Kaposi's sarcoma). Other symptoms include long-lasting diarrhea (resulting from HIV damaging the intestines, and from infection with a variety of bacterial and other pathogens) and rapid weight loss (a consequence of diarrhea or poor absorption of nutrients from the damaged intestines). Persistent, profound fatigue is also common in people with AIDS (due to infection, poor eating habits, side effects of medicine, or chronic activation of the immune system). Sores on the skin or mucous membranes (which may be caused by herpes infections) are another frequent symptom. Long-term lymph node swelling (a consequence of HIV infection itself, other infections, or cancer) and frequent fevers (typically caused by underlying bacterial infections[8]) are also symptoms associated with AIDS.

The infections that people develop vary in different parts of the world. In the United States, for example, characteristic infections that develop early in the progression of AIDS include thrush, herpes zoster (shingles), and oral hairy leukoplakia (induced by the Epstein-Barr virus, the cause of mononucleosis). In parts of Africa, active tuberculosis and malaria are among the more common and more serious infections in people with AIDS.

The underlying feature of all these diseases is a dramatic depression in the immune response of the person with AIDS. One measure of immune function is the concentration of white blood cells in the bloodstream. A particular type of

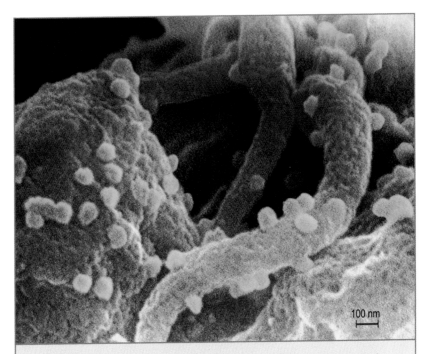

100 nm

Figure 1.3 A scanning electron micrograph of HIV (green, spherical) bound to a human lymphocyte (pink). (Centers for Disease Control and Prevention)

white blood cell, called a CD4+ T-cell, is normally present at a concentration of about 1,200 cells per microliter. (A microliter is a tiny drop, a unit of volume equivalent to one millionth of a liter, or about three ten-thousands of an ounce.) In a person with advanced AIDS, the T-cell count may drop to less than 25 cells per microliter. With low concentrations of white blood cells, the body has a very limited ability to fight infections, and this opens the door to a wide array of maladies. This immunodeficiency can be so profound that even microbes that are generally regarded as safe, such as baker's yeast, can sometimes establish an infection in people with AIDS.[9]

AIDS DEMENTIA AND RELATED DISORDERS

Symptoms associated with damage to the central nervous system are evident in about 60% of HIV-infected individuals.[10] AIDS dementia is one extreme of the spectrum of nervous system disorders, resulting in substantial memory loss and little remaining cognitive function. HIV is the most common cause of dementia in individuals younger than 60 in the United States. Prior to the development of successful treatments, about one-third of AIDS patients developed dementia. Currently, that figure is around 10%, since most AIDS patients in the United States now use effective antiretroviral treatment. Signs of modest cognitive impairment in AIDS patients have now become more common, accounting for most of the 60% of HIV-infected individuals who develop some type of neurological problem. These less-severe forms of neurological dysfunction resulting from HIV infection include mild neurocognitive disorder (MND) and asymptomatic neurocognitive impairment (ANI). MND refers to symptoms that result in some reduction in mental functioning, which affects a person's ability to carry on everyday activities. ANI refers to a loss of mental function based on psychological tests, but which is not severe enough to have a significant effect on typical daily functioning.[11]

Although nerve cells are typically not infected with HIV, other cells of the central nervous system, such as **microglial** cells and macrophages, are readily infected. (Microglial cells are **phagocytic cells** in the central nervous system that are an important component of the immune response in the brain.) These infected cells produce viral proteins that leak out and directly damage nearby nerve cells. At least three HIV proteins—**Env**, **Tat**, and **Vpr**—interact with nerve cells and damage or kill the nerves. Therefore, one mechanism of nervous system damage is the direct effects of several HIV proteins that originate from infected cells in the brain and spinal cord.

An indirect cause of damage to the central nervous system results from **inflammation**. Inflammation is a general, heightened response of the immune system to foreign material, such as HIV, in the body. While inflammation has a potential protective function in fighting some infections, the chronic inflammation that occurs with HIV infection can also be destructive. One element of inflammation is the release of chemicals called **cytokines**, which marshal the immune system to attack an invader. Some of these cytokines, particularly when present at high levels for long periods of time (as occurs with HIV infection), can directly damage the nerve cells. As a consequence, mental functioning declines. The extent of the decline depends on the degree to which nerve cells have been damaged or destroyed, either through inflammation or through the direct effects of HIV proteins.

TRANSMISSION OF THE VIRUS

HIV is transmitted through direct contact with body fluids from an infected individual. Some body fluids, like tears and saliva, contain little if any of the virus, and are unlikely to be a source of infection. Other body fluids, like blood and semen, potentially contain high levels of HIV and are effective vehicles for transmitting disease.

The primary routes of transmission of the virus are through sexual contact, exchange of blood, and childbirth and breast-feeding. Both heterosexual and homosexual sexual relations can result in transmission of HIV. Some behaviors, such as unprotected anal sex, have a higher risk of transmission than other practices. Abstinence and sexual relations with only a confirmed uninfected partner are the only certain ways of preventing sexual transmission. The use of **condoms** can also substantially reduce the likelihood of infection.

HIV is found at high concentrations in the bloodstream, and therefore it can be transmitted anytime blood is exchanged. Before the cause of AIDS was known, blood transfusions were a common cause of infection. Transmission of HIV through blood and blood products is almost unknown in developed countries, because blood is extensively tested in these locations. In some less-developed countries, blood is not rigorously screened for pathogens, so some HIV transmission still occurs through blood transfusion. Another major source of blood-borne transmission is through sharing of contaminated

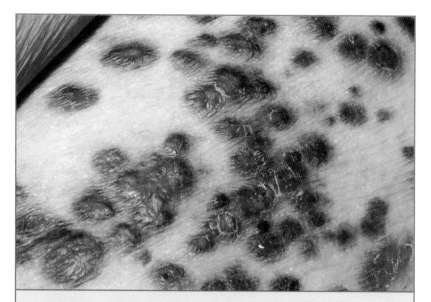

Figure 1.4 **Kaposi's sarcoma on the skin of an AIDS patient. (National Cancer Institute)**

needles. This occurs primarily in users of injectable illegal drugs. It also occurs in some less-developed countries where needles for medical procedures are reused without sterilizing them between patients.

Transmission of HIV from infected mothers to their babies appears to occur primarily shortly before or during childbirth. Delivery through caesarean section dramatically reduces the risk of HIV infection in the infant, as does taking anti-retroviral drugs during the last stages of pregnancy. HIV can also be transmitted via breast milk. It is therefore imperative that pregnant women be tested for HIV infection, so they do not transmit infection to their children.

MORBIDITY AND MORTALITY

AIDS is a devastating disease responsible for over 25 million deaths to date and about 2 million new deaths each year. One measure of the toll a disease takes is called **disability-adjusted life years (DALY)**. The DALY measure takes into account premature mortality as well as time spent in a disabled status. In 2004, the World Health Organization reported that AIDS was responsible for 58.5 million DALYs lost across the globe. This represented about 4% of the total DALYs. The World Health organization projects this will grow to 62.6 million DALYs in 2015, remaining at about 4% of the total. Another method used to measure the burden of disease is **years of life lost (YLL)**. This is an estimate of how long a person would have lived if he or she had not been afflicted with a disease. In 2004, the World Health Organization estimated that there were about 52.4 million years of life lost worldwide due to AIDS.[12]

A 2005 report from researchers at the Centers for Disease Control and Harvard University showed nearly a million DALYs lost to AIDS in 1996 in the United States, but by 1998 this had declined to about half that value. YLLs decreased from about 750,000 in 1996 to approximately 300,000 in 1998. This reflected the widespread use of effective drug therapy starting

OPERATION INFEKTION

AIDS was used as a propaganda tool for the intelligence services in the former Soviet Union and Eastern Europe. During the 1980s, these agencies disseminated information accusing the United States of developing HIV as a biological weapon, and testing the effects of the virus on unwitting prisoners. Letters to the editor or articles in newspapers and magazines were among the vehicles for disinformation. Although this campaign was eventually acknowledged and repudiated by Yevgeny Primakov, the Russian foreign intelligence director in 1992, and by agents in the East German intelligence services,[13] the story developed a life of its own. In 2005, for example, a RAND Corporation study indicated that 25% of African Americans living in the United States thought HIV was created in a government laboratory.[14] A study published in 2008 demonstrated that conspiracy theories about AIDS remain prevalent in Africa as well.[15]

in about 1996, which greatly reduced both disability and death due to AIDS.[16]

EVIDENCE THAT HIV CAUSES AIDS

There is scientific consensus that HIV causes AIDS. The evidence linking HIV and AIDS is overwhelming, and has expanded greatly since the identification of the virus in 1983–1984.

However, from the time HIV was discovered, there were people who questioned the connection between HIV and AIDS. These individuals have made claims that AIDS is primarily caused by:

- homosexual sex

- illegal drug use

- repeated exposure to foreign proteins in hemophiliacs receiving clotting factors

- the drugs used to treat HIV

- poor sanitation and health care

Several books and many Web sites on the Internet continue to advance these false claims.[17] However, all reputable scientists with expertise in viruses and HIV conclude that HIV is the cause of AIDS. Listed below is a response to specific claims that deny a link between AIDS and HIV, and details of experiments and observations that confirm a link between the virus and AIDS. A more extensive description of the evidence that HIV causes AIDS is given in a reference from the National Institutes for Allergy and Infectious Disease.[18]

Claim: Other factors, such as homosexual sex and recreational drug use, are responsible for AIDS, not HIV.

Evidence refuting the claim: Scientists at the National Institutes of Health and Johns Hopkins University tracked over 2,200 HIV-negative, homosexual men for up to nine years.[19] In this group, no unexplained cases of low CD4+ T-cell counts were found. (Low CD4+ T-cell counts are one of the critical indications that a person is beginning to develop AIDS.) Similarly, physicians at the Beth Israel Medical Center in New York showed that intravenous drug users, in the absence of HIV, did not tend to have low CD4+ T-cell counts.[20] A more definitive study tracked 715 homosexual men for over eight years. These men had similar patterns of behavior, but differed in whether they were HIV negative or HIV positive. Only individuals who were HIV positive developed AIDS (365 HIV positive, 136 AIDS cases in this group). None of the HIV negative men developed AIDS.[21] As another example, the Multicenter AIDS Cohort Study and the Women's Interagency HIV Study (WIHS) tracked over 8,000 people starting with an initial group of 5,000 in 1984. Individuals who were HIV positive were 1,100 times more likely to contract an AIDS-related illness compared to individuals in the study who were HIV negative.[22] The results from these studies, and others, strongly support a link between HIV infection and AIDS.

Claim: Hemophiliacs develop AIDS due to components in the clotting factor they received, not because of HIV.

Evidence refuting the claim: Researchers at a hospital in London compared 17 hemophiliacs who were HIV positive with 17 hemophiliacs who were HIV negative. Pairs of patients—one patient HIV positive, one patient HIV negative— were matched based on similar amounts of clotting factor used over a number of years. The 17 HIV negative hemophiliacs had no AIDS-related illness between 1980 and 1990. In contrast, between 1980 and 1990, four of the HIV positive hemophiliacs died from AIDS, and nine of the 17 had been diagnosed with AIDS.[23] A number of other scientific studies have also demonstrated no connection between exposure to proteins in clotting factor and AIDS.[24] In addition, since 1985, when clotting factors were treated to inactivate HIV, there have been essentially no new infections in hemophiliacs.[25] Yet these treatments didn't change the composition of the clotting factors themselves.

Claim: AIDS is caused by the drugs used to treat HIV infection, not the virus itself.

Evidence refuting the claim: Probably the strongest evidence against this claim is the effect newer drug treatments have on reducing levels of HIV in the blood of infected patients and delaying the onset of AIDS symptoms. For example, researchers from Europe reported that the incidence of AIDS-related illnesses in HIV positive patients declined 15-fold between 1994 and 1998 following the introduction of effective drug treatments.[26] These reductions in symptoms are directly connected with the lower levels of HIV in these patients. Patients on a three-drug regimen to treat HIV had a substantial reduction in the amount of HIV in their blood. In addition, fewer of these patients developed AIDS or died, compared to patients who used a less-effective treatment regimen.[27]

Claim: There is no direct evidence that HIV causes AIDS.

Evidence refuting the claim: One of the key ideas in medical microbiology is a set of guidelines for demonstrating that a particular microbe causes a disease. These guidelines are called **Koch's postulates**, and they delineate a set of procedures that establish the cause of an illness. Koch's postulates are a challenging prospect for HIV and AIDS because of the lack of an animal model that exactly mimics the disease in humans, and the long incubation period (a decade or more) that often elapses between infection and disease. Demonstrating Koch's postulates involves isolating a potential cause of disease, then putting the disease-causing microbe into an uninfected animal, determining if the animal develops the disease, and then re-isolating the original microbe. If all these steps are demonstrated, this is very strong evidence that the microbe in question causes the disease. The first clear evidence of HIV meeting Koch's postulates as the cause of AIDS was based on analysis of three laboratory workers that developed very low CD4+ T-cell counts following accidental infection with purified HIV. One of these workers developed an AIDS-defining illness, **Pneumocystis pneumonia**. In another example, six patients of a Florida dentist with AIDS became HIV infected with the same virus strain that infected the dentist. Five of these individuals had no other risk factor for AIDS aside from the medical procedures performed by the dentist.[28] Laboratory experiments also have shown that HIV and related viruses cause reduced immune function in several animal models, including mice that have been engineered to contain several elements of the human immune system.[29]

2

The History of HIV/AIDS

Pneumocystis pneumonia (PCP) was, prior to the 1980s, a rare infection that only affected people with a serious immune deficiency. People who developed PCP included those with a genetic defect in their immune response, certain cancer patients who received chemotherapy that damaged their immune systems, transplant patients who took immunosuppressive drugs, and young children whose immune systems were compromised due to malnutrition. A technician at the Centers for Disease Control, Sandra Ford, was in charge of fulfilling prescriptions for an experimental drug to treat PCP. She notified her supervisor on April 28, 1981, of an unusual pattern of drug requests for individuals who were not in the normal high-risk groups for PCP.[1] This new outbreak of PCP became public a few weeks later in the June 5, 1981, issue of Morbidity and Mortality Weekly Report, *which described five cases of PCP in homosexual men in Los Angeles.[2] These men were in their late twenties or thirties, and had been mostly healthy prior to their bout of pneumonia. Three of the men were tested for their immune responses, and all three showed serious immune deficits. Two of the five men had died of PCP at the time of the report. This publication marked the official start of the AIDS epidemic, although it would take over two years before the* **infectious** *agent, HIV, was identified with certainty.*

AIDS is a disease that emerged as a cause of human illness and death in the recent past. In a matter of a few decades, AIDS has spread around the world, and become a major health problem. Yet, like many current problems, HIV/AIDS has roots that extend far back in time.

HIV AND AIDS BEFORE THE 1980s

The history of HIV and AIDS prior to the 1980s is murky. There is definitive evidence that a man from the Congo in Africa was infected with HIV in 1959. This was based on an analysis of a preserved blood sample taken that year, which showed the presence of HIV, both through antibody testing[3] and analysis of DNA sequences.[4] Because so few blood samples from Africa remain from the 1950s and earlier, testing to determine the extent of HIV infection in humans during this time is not possible. However, analysis of the DNA from the 1959 blood sample and DNA from other HIV isolates suggest that HIV had been circulating in humans for decades before then.[5]

The real history of HIV requires initially shifting the focus from humans to chimpanzees. There is substantial evidence that humans acquired HIV from butchering and eating chimpanzees. The chimpanzees, based on evidence from detailed genetic analysis of the chimpanzee virus (simian immunodeficiency virus [SIV_{cpz}]), probably acquired the precursors of HIV from two different species of monkeys. There is controversy as to when chimpanzees may have acquired SIV from the monkeys. Some reports suggested that this may have occurred within the past 500 years or so. Another analysis, based in part on a study of monkey SIVs from an island off the coast of Africa, put the timing of the first chimpanzee infection with monkey SIV at about 22,000 years ago.[6]

Based on the variation in the genetics of different strains of HIV, humans probably acquired HIV from chimpanzees in the 1930s, although there is still substantial uncertainty about the timing of virus entry into the human population.[7] It may well have been that humans who hunted chimpanzees in remote areas had contracted HIV many times before the 1930s, but because travel was so infrequent from these regions to more populated areas, the disease never spread past the initial cases. It is also apparent that some adaptation was required in order for the virus to efficiently infect humans. Comparison of chimpanzee SIV sequences with HIV sequences shows key changes that likely made HIV a successful pathogen. One key natural antiviral protein in humans is tetherin. This protein typically latches on to viruses, and prevents the viruses from being released from the cell. A protein in HIV, called Vpu, interferes with human tetherin. The sequence of this protein is different in chimpanzee SIV, and it does not have the same effect: SIV Vpu does not inactivate chimpanzee tetherin. Another change in a protein is in the HIV **Gag** gene. There is a single amino acid substitution found in all HIV Gag proteins, but not found in any SIV Gag genes. This suggests a strong selective pressure in humans to drive and maintain these HIV mutations, but it is not clear what drove these genetic changes. However, based on the evidence from HIV and SIV DNA sequences, it appears that important genetic changes needed to occur before HIV became an efficient human pathogen.[8]

AIDS probably festered in Africa for several decades until, by virtue of greater travel and contact with people from other parts of the world, infected individuals spread the disease to other areas. There is also evidence that medical injections in Africa, frequently using unsterile needles, may have contributed to the rapid dissemination of AIDS during the 1950s and 1960s.[9] The original importation of the virus from Africa to the Western Hemisphere probably occurred in Haiti in the late 1960s. From there, within a year or two, HIV probably reached the United States. At the time, large numbers of Haitians were working in the Congo, and some of these individuals apparently brought the virus with them when they returned home. This conclusion is based primarily on the greater genetic diversity of HIV in Haiti, suggesting a longer period of the virus circulating in the population than in other parts of the Americas.[10] Because there is frequently a long lag between infection and outward signs of disease, it took another decade or so before AIDS was recognized. The initial clue to a new epidemic of infectious disease was the presence of Pneumocystis pneumonia in young men.

Figure 2.1 **The virus we now call HIV likely originated in chimpanzees in Cameroon in west-central Africa, as SIV (simian immunodeficiency virus), which likely was acquired when humans butchered chimpanzees for meat. (© Shutterstock)**

MAJOR DEVELOPMENTS IN HIV/AIDS IN THE 1980s

In 1981, the first cases of this new immune deficiency were reported. In 1982, the Centers for Disease Control introduced the term *acquired immune deficiency syndrome,* and that year an infant in the United States developed AIDS from a blood transfusion. This was the first known case of HIV transmitted through blood. Infants have a more rapid progression from HIV infection to the development of AIDS, so it is not surprising that a baby was the first case of AIDS caused by a blood transfusion.

Although there is not much about HIV that can be considered good news, it is a fortunate coincidence that the virus emerged at the "right" time. HIV is quite different from most viruses, and the methods needed to study this pathogen only became available shortly before AIDS burst on the scene. If HIV had become widespread in the 1950s or 1960s, it would have been decades before the tools even existed to identify the virus. This likely would have led to even more widespread infection and death due to AIDS than has occurred in the past several decades.

Among the tools needed to identify HIV was an assay for an enzyme (a protein that performs a chemical reaction) called reverse transcriptase. Reverse transcriptase converts RNA to DNA, an unusual chemical reaction. The presence of reverse transcriptase is a marker for retroviruses, and this assay aided in the identification of HIV. This enzyme was discovered and the assay developed in 1970 by Howard Temin at the University of Wisconsin–Madison, and David Baltimore at the Massachusetts Institute of Technology.[11] Recognizing the importance of this discovery, these scientists were awarded the Nobel Prize in Physiology or Medicine in 1975.

Another key development that was crucial in identifying HIV was a system for growing retroviruses in the laboratory. In the 1970s, only a few years before the first cases of AIDS, Robert Gallo's laboratory at the National Institutes of Health had devised techniques for growing a specific type of white blood cell (T-cells) in culture. This development was critical for allowing cultivation and identification, since HIV is quite finicky and will only replicate in certain types of cells.[12] In addition, by 1982 Gallo's laboratory had also isolated and identified retroviruses as a cause of human disease. This discovery paved the way for an understanding that AIDS could also be caused by a retrovirus.[13]

These techniques and the conceptual framework allowed several groups to quickly isolate and identify the virus. The first report of a new virus that was associated with AIDS came from a group of French researchers at the Pasteur Institute and two hospitals in Paris. Their report,[14] published in May 1983, showed that a retrovirus was present in the blood of a person with enlarged lymph nodes (a condition that is often a precursor to AIDS) and that the virus had characteristics expected of the cause of AIDS.

Subsequently, a flurry of publications followed in 1984, some from the French group, some from Robert Gallo's group at the National Institutes of Health in the United States, and one from a University of California scientist. These papers provided key pieces of the link between the virus and AIDS.[15] This information included the isolation of what is now called HIV from a large collection of patients and the production of clear electron microscope images of the virus, which helped classify it. These reports also showed that the virus grew to high levels in a type of human immune system cell called a CD4+ T-cell, and eventually killed those cells. The ability to isolate and grow the virus in culture allowed for the development of a blood test, which became available in 1985. It was now possible to screen and discard blood that was tainted with HIV. It also became possible to identify people who did not show disease symptoms, but were infected with HIV. Consequently, the blood test was a critical factor in helping to reduce HIV transmission.

A related virus, now called HIV-2, was identified in 1986. To date, this virus primarily infects people in West Africa and India. Infected people do sometimes develop AIDS, but the virus seems to damage the immune system at a slower rate compared to HIV-1.[16] In 1987, AZT became available to treat HIV infection. This drug was originally developed in 1964 to treat cancer.

MAJOR DEVELOPMENTS IN HIV/AIDS IN THE 1990s
By 1992, AIDS was the leading cause of death in men from 25 to 44 in the United States. Two years later, AIDS was the leading cause of death for both men and women ages 25 to 44 in the United States.

In 1993, the **polymerase chain reaction** (PCR) was developed. This eventually led to a diagnostic test for HIV that allowed detection of the virus sooner after a person was infected, as compared with the blood test described above. It became clear in 1996 that HIV used other molecules for entry into cells (chemokine receptors like CCR5 and CXCR4). Previously, CD4, a molecule on the surface of certain T-cells, was the only known receptor for HIV. This discovery of co-receptors opened the door to a better understanding of the process of cell infection, and eventually led to new treatments for AIDS.[17]

A key milestone in the battle with HIV was the development of effective drugs. The widespread use of these treatments beginning in 1996 led to a rapid drop in disease symptoms and death from AIDS. These drug regimens involve the use of at least three anti-HIV medications and are called **highly active anti-retroviral treatment** (HAART) because they dramatically reduce HIV replication in most patients. By 1996, largely due to the effectiveness of these drugs, HIV/AIDS was no longer the leading cause of death for people age 25 to 44 in the United States. A year later, in 1997, AIDS deaths were reduced over 40% in the United States compared to the prior year, primarily due to improved treatments.

MAJOR DEVELOPMENTS IN HIV/AIDS IN THE 2000s

In 2001, the U.S. Food and Drug Administration (FDA) approved the first diagnostic test for HIV based on detecting HIV RNA using the polymerase chain reaction (PCR), 18 years after this technique was first developed. Although the death rate due to HIV had improved dramatically in developed countries, in 2002 AIDS remained the leading cause of death worldwide among people age 15 to 59. In addition, in 2002, a rapid test for AIDS was approved by the FDA, which could be administered outside a clinical laboratory. This provided more access for patients interested in being tested in doctor's offices, clinics, and other settings without a laboratory.

(continues on page 34)

RETROVIRUSES AND REVERSE TRANSCRIPTASE

Retroviruses reverse the normal flow of genetic information and convert their genetic material, RNA, to DNA. In most of biology, the information flow is exclusively from DNA to RNA. This reverse information flow was first proposed by Howard Temin in the 1950s but was not widely accepted for two decades.[18]

The enzyme that converts RNA to DNA is called reverse transcriptase (transcription is the process of converting the information in DNA to RNA). The enzyme has unusual properties that are critical for survival of the virus. A key part of the viral life cycle is the insertion of a DNA copy of the viral RNA into the genome. Reverse transcriptase produces the DNA copy needed for this critical stage of the viral life cycle. In addition, reverse transcriptase is a sloppy enzyme, with a low enough fidelity that it makes errors frequently, as often as one error in a thousand attempts. Since the HIV genome is about 10,000 subunits in length, this means, on average, that each virus contains up to 10 errors or mutations.[19] Often these mutations are bad for the virus, and make the virus less capable than a normal virus of making copies of itself. However, occasionally, these mutations allow the virus to be resistant to anti-retroviral drugs, to evade the host's immune system, or to acquire other properties that help ensure its survival. The high error rate of reverse transcriptase helps ensure there will be a broad collection of virus variants in each person, and in the human population as a whole, which will be capable of adapting to a wide range of conditions. This variation also makes it much harder to develop an effective vaccine.

WILL HIV CAUSE HUMANS TO EVOLVE?

Pathogens provide a strong selection for favorable human gene variations that limit or prevent the growth of the microbe. Individuals with the appropriate complement of genes will continue to survive and reproduce; those without genes that confer resistance to infection are more likely to die without having any children. Over the course of the AIDS epidemic, it is clear that some individuals have an innate (genetic) resistance to HIV infection. Consequently, it is possible that AIDS will select for particular genes, leading to further evolution of humans.

Three pieces of evidence support this contention. One piece of evidence is the observation that many other primates (monkeys, chimpanzees, and gorillas) harbor viruses very similar to HIV, yet these animals do not develop serious illness. These other primates have evolved to coexist with the virus, based largely on changes in the types of genes that determine their immune response. For example, chimpanzees appear to have experienced selection for certain genes that provide a protective immune response against HIV-like viruses.

A second piece of evidence is the discovery that the human genome is littered with the remains of many past encounters with HIV-like viruses. Up to 8% of human genomes consist of HIV-like DNA.[20] These viruses got stuck in the genome and could not get out, and some of these viruses now play important roles for humans. For example, there is evidence that some of these "dead" viruses are critical in tamping down the mother's immune response against the fetus during pregnancy.[21] The key point is that our ancestors had many encounters with retroviruses, that we survived those encounters, and our genome is scarred with evidence of those past infections.

The third piece of evidence comes from a realization that some people (perhaps about 1%) who are infected with HIV for decades do not develop AIDS, and largely keep the virus in check. Specific versions of their genes marshal a particularly effective response against HIV, and people with these genes tend to keep the virus under control.[22] These patients are called "long-term non-progressors" or "elite controllers."

HIV AND THE POLIO VACCINE

In his book and subsequent articles, Edward Hooper elaborated a hypothesis that HIV originated as a contaminating virus in preparations of oral polio vaccine that were administered in what is now the Democratic Republic of Congo, Rwanda, and Burundi.[23] The claim was made that some batches of the polio vaccine made in Africa in the late 1950s in chimpanzee cells contained SIV. These vaccines were reputed to be manufactured in chimpanzee cell cultures in the Medical Laboratory in Stanleyville, in what is now Kisangani in the Democratic Republic of Congo. This contention is largely based on interviews of African technicians who had worked in the laboratory decades earlier. When the oral polio vaccine was administered, according to this hypothesis, some individuals were infected with SIV that mutated to HIV, and these infected individuals spread the disease. Among the evidence supporting this hypothesis is a claim that there is a close match between the area with early HIV cases, and the areas where the vaccine was administered.

In general, the hypothesis that HIV originated in oral polio vaccine is not widely accepted by scientists for several reasons. The primary scientist supposedly involved in preparing the vaccine in Stanleyville in Africa, Paul Osterrieth, has denied that batches of the vaccine were prepared in his laboratory in Africa, or that chimpanzee cells were grown in culture in his laboratory, for any purpose.[24] Several colleagues, including Stanley Plotkin, support Osterrieth's contention.[25]

Additional evidence that does not support an origin of HIV in oral polio vaccine includes analysis of archived vials of vaccine, made in the United States, which did not contain SIV, HIV, or chimpanzee DNA.[26] Evidence, based on analysis of HIV sequences, suggests that the virus originated in humans in the 1930s or earlier, well before the vaccination campaign of the 1950s.

Also, chimpanzees from the local area, where Hooper claims the vaccine was prepared, have been shown not to contain SIVs directly related to HIV, indicating that cells from these animals, if they had been used to culture polio vaccine, would not have been the source of HIV.[27] In addition, SIV or HIV are not readily transmitted via the oral route, which further reduces the likelihood that oral polio vaccination caused the AIDS epidemic.

One unfortunate outcome of the claim that polio vaccine was the source of HIV has been a delay in efforts to eradicate polio. In some African countries (e.g., Nigeria) polio vaccination has been slowed, due in part to the unfounded concern that HIV may be transmitted from the vaccine.[28] While Hooper never stated that HIV is transmitted by current polio vaccines, others have extrapolated from his work to make that claim.

(continued from page 30)

In 2008, Françoise Barré-Sinoussi and Luc Montagnier received the Nobel Prize in Physiology or Medicine for the discovery of HIV. Other scientists, particularly Robert Gallo, also made substantial contributions to the characterization of HIV, but Gallo was not included among the Nobel laureates.[29] This was controversial because many scientists felt that Gallo had made important contributions to understanding the biology of HIV, which merited sharing the prize.[30]

RECENT DEVELOPMENTS

HIV/AIDS continues to be a very active research area. Consequently, there are discoveries almost daily that could lead to more effective treatments and ultimately the prevention of HIV infection. In 2010, for example, there were reports about **antibodies** that neutralize a wide variety of HIV strains, a potential harbinger of new strategies for developing a vaccine.[31] Also in 2010, there were encouraging reports about a potential new method for reducing HIV transmission using vaginal **microbiocides** that contain an anti-HIV agent,[32] and the potential value of preexposure treatment with anti-HIV drugs.[33] On the other hand, 2010 also included reports of increasingly widespread HIV infections in Eastern Europe, and flat funding for HIV treatment and prevention in developing countries.[34] With continuing setbacks in reducing HIV transmission and a lack of understanding about some basic aspects of the biology of the disease, our ability to eliminate AIDS still appears to be a distant prospect.

3

The Biology of HIV/AIDS

Teddy lived in Uganda with her family. When she was 11, her mother and father died of AIDS. She was the oldest of four children and had taken care of her mother at home before she died. Once her mother passed away, she took on the role of caregiver for her family, but she and her siblings often suffered for a lack of food. They had no income, and no relatives nearby to help them. Members of their community ostracized them as "AIDS orphans." Neighbors even took some of the few possessions that they had. Fortunately, members of the Save the Children Foundation were able to provide support for her and her siblings.[1] Unfortunately, the number of AIDS orphans continues to grow, and many of these children live in abject poverty with no one to help them. As of 2010, over 15 million children in Africa are AIDS orphans. Many of these children are in danger of becoming prostitutes or child soldiers in one of the many conflict areas in the region.[2]

EPIDEMIOLOGY OF HIV/AIDS

In the United States in 2007, approximately 1.2 million people were infected with HIV. This represents about 0.6% of the population, or slightly more than one out of every 200 people. In 1996, the last year before effective treatments became widely available, approximately 60,000 people died each year from AIDS in the United States. Subsequently, that number has gone down to about 20,000 deaths per year and remained at that level.[3]

By contrast, in South Africa, a country with one of the highest prevalence rates in the world, approximately 5.7 million people were HIV infected in 2007. This represents about 18% of the population, or nearly 1 in 5 people, infected with HIV in 2007. In South Africa, the majority of infected individuals are women, and HIV is primarily transmitted through heterosexual contact. In South Africa in 2007, there were an estimated 350,000 deaths due to AIDS. About 28% of people in need of anti-HIV therapy received it; slightly over half of HIV-infected pregnant women received anti-HIV therapy. By 2007, approximately 1.4 million children in the country were orphans because their parents died from AIDS.[4]

The contrast between HIV and AIDS in the United States and South Africa illustrates a broader trend. HIV is much more common and deadly in sub-Saharan Africa than it is in Europe and North America. This is likely due to a number of factors, particularly a lack of education about the causes of AIDS and how it is transmitted, and limited access to effective health care and expensive HAART.

THE HIV GENOME

The genome (genetic material) of HIV consists of two identical RNA molecules. The genome is bracketed by structures called **long terminal repeats**. (Long terminal repeats are similar sequences at both ends of the viral RNA.) These structures are critical for integration of HIV into the host genome and are also critical for production of the viral RNA.

The HIV genome contains a gene called *Gag* (group-associated **antigen**), which is made as a large protein and subsequently cleaved into several smaller proteins. These smaller proteins make up several structures in the mature virus. One of these proteins, called the matrix, forms the inner portion of the viral envelope. Another protein derived from the Gag gene, the capsid, forms the conical structure that surrounds the viral RNA. A third protein, the nucleocapsid, binds to the RNA. A fourth protein produced from the Gag gene is P6, a small protein that appears critical for the release of the virus from an infected cell.[5]

The *Pol* (polymerase) gene encodes the enzyme reverse transcriptase. This enzyme converts the HIV RNA to DNA.

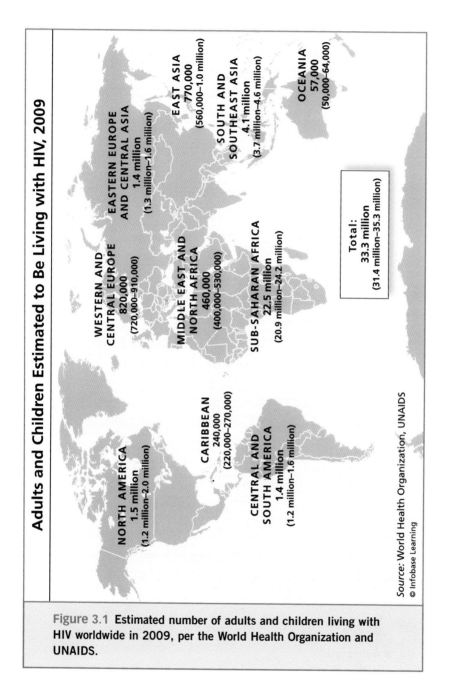

Adults and Children Estimated to Be Living with HIV, 2009

NORTH AMERICA
1.5 million
(1.2 million–2.0 million)

CARIBBEAN
240,000
(220,000–270,000)

CENTRAL AND
SOUTH AMERICA
1.4 million
(1.2 million–1.6 million)

WESTERN AND
CENTRAL EUROPE
820,000
(720,000–910,000)

EASTERN EUROPE
AND CENTRAL ASIA
1.4 million
(1.3 million–1.6 million)

MIDDLE EAST AND
NORTH AFRICA
460,000
(400,000–530,000)

SUB-SAHARAN AFRICA
22.5 million
(20.9 million–24.2 million)

EAST ASIA
770,000
(560,000–1.0 million)

SOUTH AND
SOUTHEAST ASIA
4.1 million
(3.7 million–4.6 million)

OCEANIA
57,000
(50,000–64,000)

Total:
33.3 million
(31.4 million–35.3 million)

Source: World Health Organization, UNAIDS
© Infobase Learning

Figure 3.1 Estimated number of adults and children living with HIV worldwide in 2009, per the World Health Organization and UNAIDS.

Once converted to DNA, the viral DNA can be integrated into the genome of the host cell. This enzyme is unique to retroviruses.

The *Vif* (viral infectivity factor) gene encodes a small protein likely involved in virus assembly. It is located in the interior of the virus, and probably also participates in early events in the HIV infection cycle. Viruses without Vif protein are less infectious, and do not pass easily from cell to cell, suggesting a role for Vif in virulence and transmission.[6] Vif probably increases infectiousness by blunting a key antiviral molecule in host cells, APOBEC. APOBEC normally functions by causing mutations in HIV RNA. Vif targets APOCBEC for degradation through natural cellular processes, so consequently, APOBEC is not available to fight HIV in the cell.

The *Vpr* gene encodes a protein with several critical functions in the HIV life cycle. The Vpr protein is required to move the HIV genome into the nucleus of an infected cell. This protein also contributes to cell death in infected cells, and tamps down gene expression in infected cells, which would otherwise generate a stronger immune response.

The *Rev* (regulation of virion) gene encodes a regulatory protein that allows for the export of large RNAs from the nucleus. Normally, these large RNA molecules are chopped up in the nucleus, but Rev prevents this from happening. The result is that, in the presence of the Rev protein, the RNA destined to make a new HIV particle is exported to the cytoplasm where it is packaged.

The *Tat* (transactivator of transcription) gene encodes a regulatory protein that has several key functions in the life cycle of HIV. One of its roles is the enhancement of transcription of HIV genes. It also appears to have several other roles.[7] Tat is released from infected cells and has the ability to enter other uninfected white blood cells and act as a toxin. This may be one factor in producing the loss of immune system cells that occurs in AIDS. The Tat protein may also block an important receptor on the surface of certain white blood cells. This blockage may lead to the selection of less virulent viruses early in the course of infection, and more virulent viruses at later stages of infection.[8]

The *Env* gene encodes the envelope protein, consisting of two smaller proteins, gp41 and gp120. The gp41 protein forms the "stalk" of the primary protein located in the envelope of the virus, which attaches gp120 to the virus. The gp120 protein forms a "bulb" at the end of the stalk and binds to the receptors on the surface of human cells, allowing the virus to enter those cells and establish an infection.

The **Nef** (negative factor) gene encodes a protein that plays several critical roles in the life cycle of the virus. It prolongs the life span of HIV-infected cells, thereby allowing for more virus production. It also appears to directly damage uninfected cells, thereby contributing to immunodeficiency. It may also play a role in regulating transcription of HIV genes.[9]

HIV INFECTION OF DIFFERENT HUMAN CELL TYPES

HIV primarily infects cells of the immune system, although it can also infect a variety of other cell types. In addition to infection of T-cells, B-cells, and phagocytic cells of the immune system, HIV can also infect cells lining the blood vessels, skin cells, cells lining the intestines, and heart muscle cells. HIV can also infect cells in the kidneys, liver, lungs, retina, and other organs and tissues.[10]

IMMUNE RESPONSE TO THE PATHOGEN

People who are infected with HIV have a strong immune response to the pathogen. In most cases, though, the immune response is not naturally able to prevent development of AIDS. In some cases, the immune response can actually help HIV establish and maintain infection. The ability of HIV to effectively overcome the natural human immune response makes the virus one of the most daunting challenges in medicine today.

INNATE IMMUNE RESPONSE TO HIV INFECTION

The **innate immune response** is typically a first line of defense in protection against pathogens. The cells responsible for the innate immune response typically recognize common pathogen "signatures" rather than specific molecules. For example, many pathogens (including HIV) contain particular sugars on their surface, and elements of the innate immune system recognize and react to those sugars.

Phagocytic cells are one arm of the innate immune system. These cells devour (and typically destroy) pathogens, based on their chemical signatures. Phagocytic cells include macrophages and dendritic cells. Unfortunately, these cells often are not able to destroy ingested HIV, and macrophages and dendritic cells may be among the first sites of infection when HIV is transmitted. This is likely because dendritic cells, for example, are found in and on the genitalia, where transmission of the virus frequently occurs. Phagocytic cells may play an important role in HIV infection, since they are often mobile. Once infected at one location, phagocytic cells can travel throughout much of the body and seed new sites of infection. This is particularly problematic, because these cells interact with other cells of the immune system, including CD4+ T-cells. Consequently, HIV from infected phagocytic cells may be a source of infection for other cells in the immune system. Dendritic cells and macrophage numbers typically decrease as HIV infection progresses to AIDS.[11]

Other cells of the innate immune system, such as **natural killer cells**, are also damaged or destroyed following HIV infection. Most of these effects appear to be indirect. For example, following HIV infection, the body produces fewer molecules that stimulate the activity of these cell types. The overall result is a reduction in immune system function.

A number of molecules are important components of the innate immune response. These molecules include the complement system. Complement proteins normally attach to viruses and bacteria and either lead to their direct destruction, or enhance the ability of macrophages and related cells to ingest the virus. Unfortunately, in the case of HIV, binding of complement can enhance infection since the virus targets cells like macrophages. The macrophages can more readily ingest HIV decorated with complement and once inside those cells, the virus can replicate and complete its life cycle.

ANTIBODY-BASED ADAPTIVE IMMUNE RESPONSE TO HIV INFECTION

Within one to two weeks following HIV infection, most people start producing antibodies directed against specific HIV proteins. (Antibodies are proteins produced by B-cells that bind to antigens, such as HIV proteins.) Typically, the first antibodies interact with the HIV Gag protein, and eventually high levels of antibody are produced that interact with the HIV envelope protein. Initially, antibodies are primarily found in the bloodstream, but eventually they are found in the mucosal surfaces (such as the internal lining of the genitalia) as well.

In the case of many bacterial or viral infections, the development of an antibody response leads to clearance of the pathogen, and the end of disease symptoms. Unfortunately, in the case of HIV that does not generally appear to hold.

The key regions of HIV responsible for infection are somewhat cloaked from interaction with antibodies. Consequently, most antibodies bind to accessible, but nonessential, regions of viral proteins. Mutant viruses that have a change in the shape of nonessential regions of those proteins appear at high frequency, and may no longer bind antibodies efficiently. As a result, there is a constant race between the production of antibodies and the production of new mutant viruses that can evade the antibodies. In addition, there is evidence that some of the antibodies that bind to nonessential regions block antibody access to other areas that could inactivate the virus. Consequently, the shape of the exposed viral proteins may be inducing the production of antibodies that sometimes hamper an effective immune response.

Many people infected with HIV produce antibodies that enhance the ability of the virus to infect new cells. Several types of immune system cells, such as macrophages, are able to bind antibodies that are attached to a virus. In a sense, the antibody acts as a kind of handle, allowing the macrophage to grab the virus. Therefore, in some cases, the binding of antibodies to HIV can increase the ability of the virus to enter and infect cells of the immune system. In some people it appears that HIV within their bodies mutates over time to evade the antibody response. In some cases an original HIV strain is neutralized by a particular antibody, whereas mutant strains demonstrate enhanced cell entry with the same antibody.[12]

Finally, there is evidence that, in some people, antibody production following HIV infection can eventually lead to **autoimmune disorders**. (Autoimmune disorders are diseases caused by the immune system attacking the body itself.) Autoimmunity may result from a general deregulation of B-cells, which might begin to produce larger volumes of antibodies directed against tissues in the body. Another element of antibody-induced autoimmunity could result from the similarity of some HIV proteins to human proteins. Antibodies directed against some of these HIV proteins could also bind the human proteins, and this may trigger an autoimmune reaction. In addition, the chronic activation of the immune system, which is typical of HIV infection, contributes to an increased likelihood of autoimmunity.[13]

It therefore appears that the production of antibodies following HIV infection is a delicate balance. On the one hand, it is possible for B-cells to produce antibodies that neutralize HIV and help prevent infection. On the other hand, mutations in the virus can prevent the antibodies from working and can even enhance the ability of the virus to infect new cells. The antibody response may also lead to autoimmunity, and this has implications both for the course of infection in a patient, as well as the development of vaccines, which typically stimulate antibody-based immune responses.[14]

CELLULAR ADAPTIVE IMMUNE RESPONSE

Another key area of the **adaptive immune response** are cells (such as **CD8+ T-cells**) that destroy virus-infected cells. In many viral diseases, CD8+ T-cells (**cytotoxic T-lymphocytes** or CTLs) are critical for the termination of infection. In the case of HIV, the virus has a number of strategies that allow it to evade this important branch of the immune system.

Normally, CD8+ T-cells recognize a particular stretch of a pathogen protein, which is stuck on the outside surface of an infected cell (**antigen presentation**). This recognition triggers the CD8+ T-cell to release chemicals that destroy the infected cell and allow the viruses hidden inside to be destroyed by the immune system.

With HIV infection, a number of factors can disrupt this normal immune response. For example, mutation of the stretch of viral protein recognized by the CD8+ T-cell can lead to immune system evasion. In addition, the virus can reduce the efficiency of antigen presentation on infected cells. Consequently, the CTL immune response of CD8+ T-cells often does not play a major role in limiting HIV infection and the development of AIDS.

There is also evidence that CTL action might exacerbate the effects of HIV infection. For example, CTLs in HIV-infected patients can destroy uninfected CD4+ T-cells. These CTLs can also destroy other immune system cells, such as antigen-presenting cells. Chimpanzees, which do not develop a CTL response to similar viruses, remain disease free.[15] This observation leads to questions about the role of CD8+ T-cells in the immune response to HIV.

THE IMMUNOPATHOGENESIS OF HIV INFECTION

HIV infection typically induces a strong (although ineffective) immune response. There is increasing evidence that this chronic, elevated immune response is one factor that contributes to the illnesses associated with HIV infection. This revved

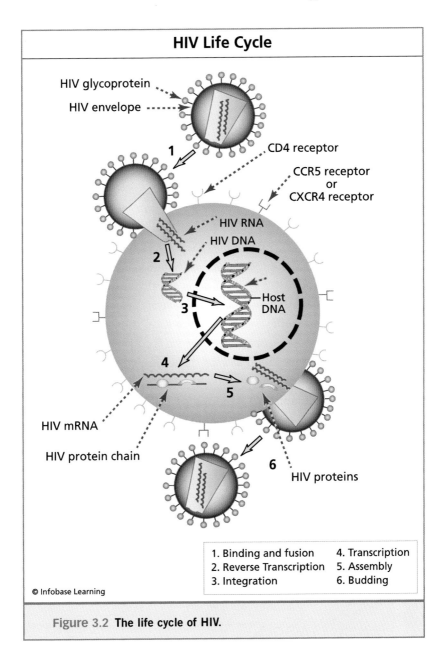

HIV Life Cycle

HIV glycoprotein

HIV envelope

CD4 receptor

CCR5 receptor
or
CXCR4 receptor

1

HIV RNA

HIV DNA

2

3

Host
DNA

4

5

HIV mRNA

HIV protein chain

6

HIV proteins

1. Binding and fusion   4. Transcription
2. Reverse Transcription 5. Assembly
3. Integration   6. Budding

© Infobase Learning

Figure 3.2 **The life cycle of HIV.**

up immune response has a number of effects. For example, many different antibody-producing B-cells are activated, T-cells are produced and die off at high levels, and the levels of chemical messengers (cytokines) that activate cells of the immune system are elevated.

From the point of view of the virus, chronic activation of the immune system is likely to be beneficial, because activated T-cells are the site of virus replication. However, from the point of view of the infected person, this chronic activation has many detrimental effects. After long-term activation of the immune system, many of the key organs and immune systems start to break down. For example, the thymus is an organ that plays a key role in the maturation of immune system cells. In people with progressive HIV infection the thymus often loses its function, likely due to damage from chronic inflammation. Similarly, lymph nodes, which play a critical role in immune response to pathogens, become filled with scar tissue following chronic immune activation and lose their effectiveness as a site for aiding immune responses.

The chronic immune activation by HIV likely has other consequences as well. The gastrointestinal tract contains a wide variety of immune system cells. It appears that HIV does a great deal of damage to those cells, and this, in turn, leads to overall dysfunction of the gut. This may be responsible for the common observation that people with AIDS frequently present with weight loss and chronic diarrhea. Among the consequences of damage to the gastrointestinal tract is the leakage of bacterial products into the bloodstream, which can further activate the immune system, and cause further damage to cells and tissues of the immune system.[16]

VIRULENCE FACTORS

Any pathogen must have strategies to evade the host immune response in order to infect a host. HIV is no exception. A number of HIV proteins act as **virulence factors** to suppress or evade the immune response. (Virulence factors are components of a pathogen that allows the pathogen to cause disease, often through immune system evasion.)

One example is the HIV Tat protein. Although a key function of Tat is the activation of HIV transcription, this protein also has the potential to interact with a number of elements of the host immune response.[17] For example, Tat is known to cause white blood cells to increase the number of CCR5 and CXCR4 molecules on their surface. Since these molecules are important receptors facilitating HIV entry, Tat expression likely increases the susceptibility of white blood cells to infection. Tat has also been demonstrated to inhibit replication of antibody-producing B-cells, and to increase the production of **IL-10** by another type of white blood cell. IL-10 is a cytokine, a chemical messenger between immune system cells. IL-10 is a signal to shut down immune responses, so Tat induction of IL-10 would tend to dampen host immunity. Tat has also been shown to block natural killer cell activity, a component of the innate immune response that otherwise might be help control HIV replication.

Another example of a virulence factor is the HIV Nef protein. Nef has a number of functions in viral entry, replication, and exit from the host cell. Nef also interacts with the immune system in several ways to reduce the effectiveness of the immune response to HIV infection. Nef decreases the expression of **major histocompatability class I (MHC class I)** on the surface of infected cells. (MHC class I is a molecule that presents antigens from intracellular pathogens on the surface of antigen-presenting cells.) This reduces the presentation of antigen, thereby making the virus-infected cells hidden from immune surveillance. Like Tat, Nef can also induce the production of IL-10, thereby putting an overall damper on the immune response. Nef also promotes the death of uninfected bystander cells, including cytotoxic T-lymphocytes, through a process called **apoptosis** (programmed cell death). Since these cells are critical for a vigorous immune response, their loss is a major blow in fighting infection.[18]

The HIV Env protein also has a number of negative effects on the host immune response. It is toxic to T-cells, causing an increase in the rate of cell death, and reducing normal immune responses of T-cells. Env, like Nef and Tat, induces IL-10, causing overall immune system suppression. Env also causes the production of IL-4, resulting in B-cells producing IgE, a type of antibody that is associated with allergy and inflammation.

Overall, various HIV proteins have a powerful, negative effect on the immune response of both individual cells, as well

ANIMAL MODELS FOR STUDYING HIV/AIDS

One of the major challenges in studying HIV/AIDS is the lack of an animal model that closely approximates AIDS in humans. Much research on HIV has been conducted on cells growing in culture in the laboratory. While this work has helped in understanding cellular infection and the role various HIV genes play in the life cycle of the virus, it does not come close to mimicking the complexity of the interplay of the virus and the immune system in the body.

Various primates have been studied as models for HIV infection and the development of AIDS. The primary models have been chimpanzees and macaques. Chimpanzees can be infected with HIV, and some of the infected chimps do develop some symptoms of immune deficiency. However, chimpanzees do not develop full-blown AIDS, and the expense and ethical issues surrounding infectious disease work on this endangered species have made HIV/AIDS studies with chimps increasingly rare.

A more commonly used animal model has been macaques. These monkeys are not endangered, and a number of research as the immune system as a whole. This is on top of the damage caused by destruction of the CD4+ T-cells by HIV.

HUMAN GENETIC FACTORS THAT AFFECT HIV INFECTION AND PROGRESSION TO AIDS

A number of observations have demonstrated that individuals have different susceptibility to HIV infection and progression to AIDS. These observations include small numbers of commercial sex workers who remained uninfected after multiple exposures to HIV, and elite controllers who have been infected

facilities have large colonies of the monkeys available for research. One of the drawbacks of using macaques is that these monkeys are not readily infected with HIV. Instead, most experiments with macaques involve a related virus, SIV, or an SIV/HIV hybrid virus. Consequently, it is not always clear how the results from these experiments apply to HIV in humans. However, recent work has allowed for the use of only slightly modified HIV to establish infection in macaques, so this animal model may become even more important in the future.[19]

Another important animal model are mice that have been modified to house components of the human immune system. While these mice have proven useful in a variety of experiments designed to test the efficacy of anti-HIV treatments and to answer other questions related to the biology of HIV, they do not contain the full range of human immune functions and organs.[20] Consequently, there are limitations on the extent to which the results from mice with components of a human immune system translate back to human disease.

for years, even decades, without progressing to AIDS. In some cases, these individuals have genetic differences that provide some protection against HIV. Other individuals appear to harbor genetic differences that result in more rapid progress to AIDS following infection.

GENETIC FACTORS ASSOCIATED WITH RESISTANCE OR SUSCEPTIBILITY TO HIV

The human leukocyte antigen (HLA, also known as MHC) is a key element of the immune system. HLAs are proteins that present sections of pathogen proteins (antigens), which, in

ELITE CONTROLLERS

In a long-term study of individuals with HIV infection, 15% of individuals were clinically healthy 10–15 years after HIV infection, and 4% of the group had normal levels of CD4+ T-cells in their blood and low levels or undetectable levels of HIV.[21] This group is called "elite controllers" and they have been studied extensively in hopes of gaining insight into how they prevent the normally devastating effects of HIV infection. Studies to date suggest a variety of factors that are responsible for the ability of these individuals to successfully fight infection.

One factor is genetic. It appears that elite controllers are more likely to have genes that are better able to recognize and destroy HIV-infected cells. Some elite controllers, for example, have mutations in CCR5, which make it harder for the virus to enter their cells.

A second factor responsible for some elite controllers is infection with defective virus strains. Some of these strains, for example, lack a functional Nef gene. This is interesting in light of the consideration of Nef-deleted virus as a vaccine. There are also reports of Vif mutations in human turn, help activate the immune response to fight the microbial invader. HLA genes are highly variable between individuals. Some HLA variants can more effectively present HIV antigens that provide protection; some HLA variants are less effective at presenting protective antigens. Consequently, some HLA variants contribute to protection from HIV infection, while other variants contribute to HIV susceptibility.[22]

A critical factor in HIV entry into human cells is the presence of co-receptors, including CCR5. Gene variants in CCR5 have been linked to protection from HIV infection. For example, a 32 base-pair deletion in the CCR5 gene, which leads

immunodeficiency viruses that have infected some elite controllers. However, a study of viruses from nearly 100 elite controllers found only a small number of mutations in Nef and other genes. Most of the genetic changes could be attributed to less intense immune selection of the viruses, or differences in circulating viruses at the time these individuals were infected. This report did not support the idea that elite controllers are generally infected with weakened viral strains.[23]

A third factor relating to HIV infection for some elite controllers is their immune response. It appears that elite controllers maintain a stronger CD8+ CTL response against HIV, as compared to those people who progress to disease. This may be tied in with the genetic factors described above. Certain combinations of genes (particularly the HLA) may favor a stronger and more appropriate immune response to HIV. In contrast, antibody-based immune responses do not appear to be a major factor in the survival of elite controllers. This information has relevance for future attempts at vaccination. Likely, a successful HIV vaccine would have to induce a strong CD8+ CTL response, rather than a vigorous antibody response.

to the absence of CCR5 protein on the surface of cells, protects against infection with HIV strains that use this co-receptor.[24]

Another gene linked to susceptibility or resistance to progression to AIDS is TRIM5α. In primates, variants of this protein are able to restrict replication of retroviruses, possibly by interfering with viral uncoating on entry into the cell. To determine if variants of human TRIM5α can play a role in controlling HIV infection, researchers at several institutes and universities in the Netherlands studied a cohort of 364 homosexual men who were either HIV infected, or became infected, between 1984 and 1986. They tracked how quickly the men developed AIDS symptoms, and linked the progression to AIDS based on variants in the TRIM5α protein. These physicians and scientists determined that one variant delayed the time between infection and high viral loads in the blood associated with AIDS, and another variant clearly accelerated the progression to high viral loads associated with AIDS.[25]

Human cyclophilin A (CypA) is a protein that has a function within normal human cells. This protein is also packaged into HIV and increases virus replication, based on experiments that showed limited HIV replication in human cells that lack CypA. Researchers from the National Cancer Institute, the University of Pittsburgh, the San Francisco Department of Health, and Johns Hopkins University identified variants in the gene that encodes the CypA protein. These scientists also determined that some of these variants were more common in individuals who progressed to AIDS faster. Therefore, genetic differences in the CypA protein may affect progression to AIDS.[26]

Other genetic variations that may contribute to resistance or susceptibility to HIV have been identified, and other important variants are likely to be found as additional genetic studies are conducted. However, it appears that fewer than 1% of people are naturally able to control progression to AIDS, so this is not likely to be a major factor in preventing the spread of the disease.[27]

CHALLENGES IN ELIMINATING THE VIRUS FROM THE BODY

A key problem in fighting HIV infection is that the virus inserts its DNA directly into the genome of infected cells. Consequently, it may never be possible to eliminate the virus once an infection has been established. Some of the cells the virus infects are very long-lived, so waiting out the virus until infected cells die has not proven to be an effective strategy. This feature of the biology of the virus, the insertion of its DNA into host cell DNA, is one of the most challenging aspects of HIV in terms of efforts to cure infected individuals, and prevent the transmission of infection to others.

DIFFERENT TYPES OF HIV

To date, three main classes of HIV (aside from HIV-2) have been identified. This includes Group M (main), which is responsible for over 99% of HIV infections, along with Group N (non-M or O) and O (outlier). Groups N and O are primarily restricted to a few cases in Africa, whereas Group M viruses are distributed around the world.

Group M viruses appear to be particularly well adapted to establishing and transmitting disease in humans, likely explaining their widespread distribution. Within the M group, there are a number of different subtypes, or clades. These subtypes include A1, A2, B, D, K, F1, F2, H, C, J, and G. Each subtype differs from the others by its molecular signature, differing by at least 20% in the envelope protein, and 15% in the Gag protein. Subtype B viruses are the predominant group in North America.

This tremendous variation of virus types complicates the development of a vaccine. Since the virus is so variable, it is challenging to develop a vaccine capable of promoting immunity to the many viral strains that exist in nature.

4

Treatment of HIV/AIDS

An AIDS patient, John, was infected with HIV in the 1980s. Like other victims of this devastating disease, he had battled a number of painful, debilitating infections over the years, but managed to recover each time. In 1995, he developed an aggressive cancer and it seemed unlikely that his body could fight against this disease for very long. However, shortly after John's cancer diagnosis, encouraging results began emerging from clinical trials involving AIDS treatments that simultaneously used multiple drugs. Once patients started these new treatment regimes, their survival rates improved dramatically. John was one of the patients who benefited from these new medications. Once he started multidrug treatment, he rapidly began to feel better, and could effectively battle his cancer. He went back to his career as an artist, and even tried scuba diving. John died in 2004, much later than would have been expected had the new HIV treatments not been developed.[1]

DIAGNOSIS OF HIV INFECTION AND AIDS

In the early days of the AIDS epidemic, unusual disease symptoms, such as Pneumocystis pneumonia, were the initial indicators that a person was infected with HIV. At the time, there was no specific test for detecting HIV. That situation changed in 1985 with the development of an antibody test for HIV infection. Subsequently, a number of additional diagnostic tests have been developed to determine if a person is HIV infected.

TESTS THAT DETECT ANTIBODIES TO HIV

The standard first test for detecting HIV is an **ELISA** (enzyme-linked immunosorbent assay). In this test, blood is taken from a patient, and the blood is centrifuged. (A **centrifuge** is a device for spinning samples at high speed.) This separates the blood cells from the liquid, called serum. The serum is then added to a plastic plate containing small wells coated with HIV proteins. If a person has been infected with HIV for at least a few weeks, the person will likely have HIV antibodies in his or her serum, and these antibodies will bind the HIV proteins in the well. This ultimately results in a color change that can be detected with a laboratory instrument. If a person has not been infected, there will be no color change in the well. The sensitivity of the test is over 99% (a measure of how likely someone who is positive is identified as positive in the test). The specificity of the test is over 98% (a measure of how likely someone who is negative is identified as negative in the test). Because of the importance of correctly determining whether someone is actually HIV infected, additional tests are typically used to confirm the ELISA results.

To confirm a positive ELISA, a **Western blot** is frequently used. This test uses a set of HIV proteins that are separated by size on a gel, and then transferred to a paper-like membrane. Serum from a patient is incubated with the membrane. If the patient has HIV antibodies, these will bind to the membrane and produce a band. The presence of at least two different bands corresponding to HIV proteins confirms an HIV-positive diagnosis.

One potential problem with the ELISA and Western blot tests is that it often takes weeks (rarely even months) from the time a person is first infected until he or she produces sufficient antibodies to be detected in these tests. This was particularly a concern with blood donations, as it meant there could be a gap between the time a person could transmit HIV and the time that an infection is detected. Consequently, additional tests are used to reduce the risk of transfusing infected blood. In addition, the standard antibody tests do not produce immediate results. In some cases, it is important to get a rapid diagnosis to determine if immediate treatment is needed. For example, if a health-care worker suffers a needlestick with a blood-contaminated needle, testing of the person on whom the needle was used can provide information on whether to provide the worker with antiretroviral medications. As another example, if a woman in labor has an unknown HIV status, a rapid HIV test could provide guidance on whether to administer antiretroviral drugs, in order to protect her child from HIV infection.

The U.S. Food and Drug Administration has approved two rapid HIV antibody tests. The OraQuick ADVANCE® Rapid HIV Test allows testing of material taken from cheek swabs or a blood sample. The Uni-Gold Recombigen™ HIV Test uses a blood sample. Results are available within 10 to 20 minutes, and the accuracy is similar to that of an ELISA tests. These tests are particularly valuable if the patient turns out to be HIV negative.

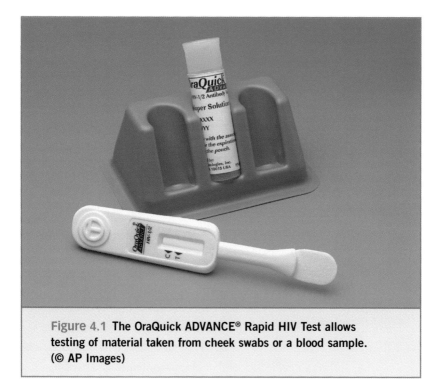

Figure 4.1 The OraQuick ADVANCE® Rapid HIV Test allows testing of material taken from cheek swabs or a blood sample. (© AP Images)

If either test gives a positive result, it must be confirmed with a Western blot.[2]

Because of the importance of testing individuals at risk for HIV infection to determine whether they are infected, several tests that can be used outside a traditional laboratory setting have been approved. One, the Home Access HIV-1 Test System, allows testing at home. The user stabs his or her finger with a sterile needle included in the kit, and returns the resulting blood sample through the mail. Results are available by telephone, with access to the results provided through a code included in the kit. The test is based on an ELISA, so positive results must be confirmed through Western blot testing or other means.

Another test, OraSure, is available in doctor's offices. It relies on collecting material with a swab from the cheek, inside the mouth. Once collected, the sample is sent to a standard laboratory for testing. Both an ELISA and Western blot is performed on the sample, and the results are as accurate as with a blood test using the same procedures.[3]

TESTS THAT DETECT HIV RNA

These alternative tests involve detecting the HIV genetic material, and are called nucleic acid tests. As a consequence, they can detect HIV within about 12 days following infection because the HIV RNA is present once infection occurs. This contrasts with the antibody tests, which detect only about 50% of HIV infections three weeks after they have occurred, since the body must produce antibodies to the virus before these tests will identify an infection.

One type of nucleic acid test uses a technique called polymerase chain reaction (PCR). PCR acts like a molecular version of a copy machine, and it is capable of detecting as few as 40 copies of HIV RNA per milliliter of blood. The test involves conversion of HIV RNA to DNA, then repeated cycles of high temperature to separate the DNA strands, lower temperature to allow small DNA primers to bind, and higher temperature to allow a special DNA polymerase (an enzyme that synthesizes DNA) to act. This process amplifies the original amount of HIV RNA about a millionfold, making it visible. The presence of HIV nucleic acid indicates that the tested material has the potential to transmit the virus.

A second type of nucleic acid test is a transcription-mediated assay. This procedure involves the isolation and capture of HIV RNA. Once the HIV is captured, it is converted to DNA, and the DNA is used as a template to make many RNA copies. These RNA copies are then detected using a DNA probe that gives off light in the presence of another chemical. If sufficient light is detected, it indicates that HIV RNA was present in the original sample, and that the sample has the potential to transmit HIV. These nucleic acid-based assays, in conjunction with antibody and donor screening, have reduced the risk of transmitting HIV through blood transfusions to 1 in 2 million in the United States.[4]

There is also another type of nucleic acid test that is used to provide data that helps improve HIV treatment. It is called **real-time (or quantitative) PCR**, and it measures the amount of HIV RNA in the blood. Through repeated testing over weeks and months, it is possible to determine whether treatment is reducing the amount of virus in the blood, a key indicator of improving health. If treatment is not lowering virus counts, it may be a sign of poor compliance with treatment or that the virus is resistant to the medications being used. This information can then be used to help design a more effective treatment protocol.

The test uses the same basic principles as standard PCR. The difference is that the reaction is conducted in such a way that the amount of amplified material is measured during each cycle of the reaction. Based on a comparison with a known set of standards that are tested at the same time, it is possible to determine the number of copies of HIV RNA present in the original sample.

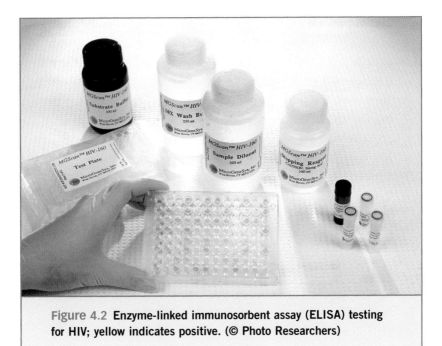

Figure 4.2 Enzyme-linked immunosorbent assay (ELISA) testing for HIV; yellow indicates positive. (© Photo Researchers)

WHEN TREATMENT SHOULD BEGIN

In a number of situations, the answer to this question is fairly clear-cut. If a patient has an illness associated with AIDS, or he or she is coinfected with hepatitis B or C virus, experts recommend administration of anti-HIV therapy right away. In addition, experts recommend that all HIV-positive women who are pregnant be given anti-HIV treatment after the first trimester, since this has been shown to dramatically reduce the risk of transmitting the virus to the infant.

There is still some controversy as to when to initiate treatment for some HIV patients. The CD4 count threshold for starting ART has changed over time, from ≤ 500, down to ≤ 250 and now back up to 500. Experts are divided on the recommendation for treatment when a patient has over 500 CD4+

T-cells per cubic millimeter of blood. In these situations, some experts recommend treatment; others recommend evaluating each patient on a case-by-case basis before making a treatment decision. As new drugs are developed and new studies are completed, it is likely that the recommendations about when to initiate anti-HIV therapy will continue to evolve.

The decision to begin HIV treatment is a commitment to lifelong adherence to a drug regimen that may cause side effects. Patients who fail to adhere to treatment run an increased risk of developing viruses that are resistant to drugs, and consequently an HIV infection that will be more difficult to control in the future.[5]

TREATMENTS FOR HIV INFECTION

One of the most dramatic developments since the first reports of AIDS has been the development of effective treatments for HIV infection. These treatments target specific stages of the viral life cycle that are unique. Consequently, these drugs hamstring the virus, while generally producing only mild or moderate side effects in the patient. These treatments, called highly active anti-retroviral therapy (HAART), were first available in 1996, and have dramatically reduced the risk of death for those with access to the drugs. The various classes of HIV antivirals are described below.

NUCLEOTIDE OR NUCLEOSIDE REVERSE TRANSCRIPTASE INHIBITORS (NRTIs)

A critical part of the viral life cycle is the conversion of viral RNA to DNA. The enzyme that catalyzes this reaction is reverse transcriptase (RT). The **nucleotide or nucleoside reverse transcriptase inhibitors** (NRTIs) are mimics of the normal building blocks of DNA. These drugs can be incorporated into a DNA chain by reverse transcriptase and prevent the chain from being further extended. This stops HIV replication in its tracks. These drugs are specific for HIV because HIV RT is naturally able to interact with and incorporate these compounds, whereas the main DNA synthesizing enzymes in cells do not interact with these drugs. This helps explains why HIV RT is selectively targeted by these compounds.[6]

These drugs are inactive when ingested. They require the action of cellular enzymes to convert them to an active compound that targets reverse transcriptase.

Examples of nucleotide or nucleoside RT inhibitors include AZT or zidovudine, the first drug approved to treat HIV infection. Other nucleoside or nucleotide RT inhibitors are abacavir, didanosine, emtricitabine, lamivudine, stavudine, and tenofovir.

These drugs can have a number of side effects, including anemia, nausea, vomiting, diarrhea, liver toxicity, potential for changes to cholesterol levels, increased risk of diabetes, and lipodystrophy (a dysfunction of fat distribution in the body—typically, following treatment, the amount of fat is reduced in the extremities, and increased around the body core). Other side effects include kidney damage, nerve damage in the feet and hands, and damage to the pancreas. Many of these effects are likely due to damage to cellular **mitochondria** (little organs inside the cells that are critical for energy metabolism). In many cases, only one or two of the nucleoside or nucleotide RT inhibitors have the side effects described. There is also evidence that some patients may develop an allergy to at least one of these drugs, and this may contribute to some of the side effects.[7]

NON-NUCLEOSIDE REVERSE TRANSCRIPTASE INHIBITORS

Non-nucleoside reverse transcriptase inhibitors (NNRTIs) hit the same target (RT) as the NRTIs but through a different mechanism that involves blocking a pocket of the RT enzyme. Insertion of an NNRTI into the pocket of the enzyme changes its shape, preventing the enzyme from making DNA.[8] Since the NNRTIs and NRTIs have a different mechanism of action,

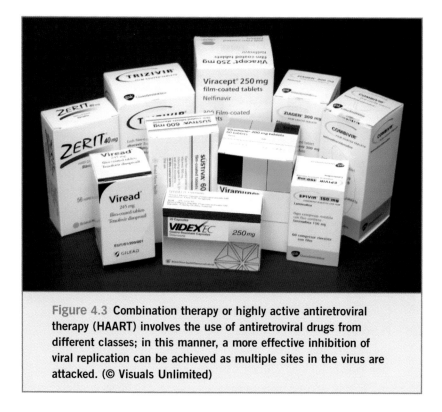

Figure 4.3 **Combination therapy or highly active antiretroviral therapy (HAART) involves the use of antiretroviral drugs from different classes; in this manner, a more effective inhibition of viral replication can be achieved as multiple sites in the virus are attacked. (© Visuals Unlimited)**

often viruses that are resistant to one class of the drugs are not resistant to the other class of drugs. Side effects from these drugs include short-term central nervous system changes such as drowsiness, insomnia, and hallucinations. There is also a risk of liver toxicity with all these agents and liver failure with one agent, nevirapine. These drugs may also cause an increase in total cholesterol levels.

PROTEASE INHIBITORS

Key HIV proteins are initially made as part of a large polyprotein. To be functional, the large polyprotein must be cleaved into smaller, functional proteins. The HIV **protease** is required for this task. Unless the protease does its job, HIV particles cannot mature and the virus cannot replicate. The U.S. Food and Drug Administration has approved a number of **protease inhibitors** for treating HIV, including atazanavir, darunavir, fosamprenavir, indinavir, lopinavir, nelfinavir, ritonavir, saquinavir, and tipranavir.

Side effects of this class of drugs include diarrhea, heart attacks and other heart illness, nausea, vomiting, liver toxicity, changes in cholesterol and lipid levels in the blood, and kidney damage. There has also been a suggestion that some of these agents might be linked to peripheral nerve damage, although the data is not yet conclusive.[9]

CELL-FUSION INHIBITOR

Among the first steps in the HIV life cycle is the virus fusing with the membrane of a cell. Interfering with this step prevents the virus from infecting new cells. Enfuvirtide is an example of a **fusion inhibitor**. Specifically, it prevents the lower portion of the envelope (gp41) from productively binding to the cell membrane. This is an essential step in the fusion process, so it prevents HIV from entering the cell.[10] This drug was approved in 2003; side effects include intestinal disturbance, dizziness, muscle pain, and insomnia.

CCR5 ANTAGONIST

HIV binds to cells through the CD4 receptor. Many HIV strains enter cells using a second receptor (a protein on the cell surface) called CCR5. This is part of the fusion process, but is a discrete step. Currently, maraviroc is the sole approved **CCR5 antagonist**; it was approved in 2007. The drug is intended for patients who harbor resistant viruses that are not readily treated with other agents. Maraviroc binds to CCR5 and changes the shape of the protein, which prevents the HIV envelope protein from interacting with CCR5, and prevents fusion of HIV with the cell.[11] Side effects have included kidney damage in some patients.

INTEGRASE INHIBITORS

HIV DNA must integrate into the genome in order for the virus to complete its life cycle. An enzyme called integrase allows the HIV DNA to insert into the cellular genome. This process also helps immortalize the virus and makes it difficult to eliminate, since integration makes the virus a permanent part of the cell it infects. Preventing integration is therefore another effective strategy in reducing the ability of HIV to replicate. Initially, it was thought that integrase would be a difficult target for drug development. The virus contains about 50 copies of the integrase protein, and only one copy needs to work one time in order for the HIV DNA to be inserted into the host cell. Fortunately, an effective integrase inhibitor was discovered and the drug, raltegravir, was approved in 2007. It is the only integrase inhibitor that is currently available. The drug interferes with the ability of the enzyme to bind metal ions that are required for integrase activity.[12] Side effects include headache, dizziness, insomnia, and gastrointestinal disturbances.

MULTIDRUG COCKTAILS

When the first drug, AZT, was approved for treating AIDS in 1987, patients who received AZT typically felt better and had fewer symptoms. However, individuals who received AZT did not have better long-term survival than those who did not take the drug.[13] The primary reason for this lack of durable drug effectiveness was viral resistance. HIV is highly mutable—on average, each virus has up to 10 mutations, as compared to the virus from which it originated. Therefore, AZT-resistant mutants were likely already present in a person's body before he or she started taking the drug. When the patient took AZT, those resistant mutants were selected and could continue to grow. Considering that each infected cell can produce up to 10,000 viruses per day,[14] HIV levels can rebound quickly.

Based on this observation, subsequent treatments involved using multiple drugs that target different steps in the viral life

cycle or different parts of the same viral enzyme. The likelihood of a single virus simultaneously developing resistance to
three drugs would be the product of the likelihood of developing resistance to each drug. Therefore, if the probability of
developing resistance is a million to one for each drug, the
probability of simultaneously developing resistance to all three
drugs is 1×10^{14}.

Common drug combinations include two NRTIs and one
NNRTI or two NRTIs and one protease inhibitor. Currently,
the preferred combination therapy consists of the NRTIs
emtricitabine and tenofovir and either the NNRTI efavirenz or
one of several protease inhibitors. This particular combination
of NRTIs is based on the observation that resistance to emtricitabine frequently results in the virus becoming sensitive to
another NRTI.[15]

Some considerations in the prescription of specific drug
combinations include choices based on minimizing side effects;
prior anti-HIV drug use; observation of resistance; pregnancy;
other medicines a patient is taking; coinfections with other
viruses (such as hepatitis B); and preexisting disease, such as
liver dysfunction. Several of the commonly used drug combinations are now available as a single pill, which makes it easier for
patients to maintain the appropriate drug regime.

TREATMENT FAILURE AND RESISTANCE

Treatment failure is defined in several different ways. *Virologic
failure* indicates that the number of viruses found in the blood
has not declined as expected. *Immunologic failure* occurs when
the number of CD4+ T-cells does not rebound after treatment.
Clinical failure means that a person's symptoms do not improve
and AIDS progresses following treatment. In many cases, all
three indications of treatment failure will occur simultaneously.
The inability to control HIV infection can result from genetic
factors in a patient that lead to low levels of medicines being
present in the body, from failure of a patient to correctly take

the medications (often due to side effects), or infection with a resistant virus. Since treatment failure often results from, or leads to, the selection of resistant viruses, determining virus resistance can be an important part of developing a new treatment plan. Therefore, resistance testing is often a key element in helping to decide which drugs a patient should take. There are two types of resistance testing: **genotypic** and **phenotypic**.

Genotypic testing involves sequencing the protease gene, and a portion of the RT gene from HIV isolates from a patient, to identify specific mutations that are known to cause **drug resistance**. While this is a relatively simple test to perform, the interpretation of a negative test is more difficult. If, for example, a drug is no longer being taken by a patient, it is possible that only a small number of resistant viruses are still present, and these may be too rare to be detected in the test. However, if that same drug is taken again, those resistant viruses will be selected, and they will rapidly increase in frequency.

The basic procedure for genotypic testing involves taking a blood sample, isolating virus RNA, performing RT-PCR, and then sequencing the resulting DNA. Compared to phenotypic testing, genotypic testing is faster and less expensive. A disadvantage of genotypic testing is that mutations need to appear at high frequency in order for them to be detected, and since the test is indirectly measuring resistance, some resistant viruses may not be identified. In the United States, there are currently two approved genotypic testing methods available (ViroSeq® and TrueGene™). Current recommendations favor genotypic testing, as compared with phenotype testing, unless the patient has a very complex pattern of resistance.[16]

Phenotypic testing involves isolating HIV RNA from patients, and converting the portion of the RNA from the protease and reverse transcriptase genes into DNA. This DNA is then inserted into a modified HIV genome, which contains a **luciferase** reporter gene. (Luciferase is an enzyme found in some bacteria and in fireflies that produces light when the

CAN TREATMENT LEAD TO A CURE?

When HAART was developed, there was hope that it could entirely eliminate HIV from the body and result in a cure for the disease. In many patients that underwent treatment, HIV levels in the blood became undetectable, so it seemed reasonable that treatment could eventually be stopped and the patient's immune system would have recovered enough to fight the virus without continuing to take the drugs.

Unfortunately, studies that tested the possibility of stopping drug treatment did not generate encouraging data. Patients that stopped taking the drugs soon had a spike in HIV levels in the blood. Aside from putting a nail in the coffin of the hypothesis that HAART could cure HIV infection, this result was a major concern because it raised the specter of drug resistance developing if patients took their drugs intermittently.

In retrospect, the inability to cure HIV with drugs was not surprising. As part of its life cycle, HIV integrates into host cell DNA. Therefore, a patient will continue to harbor many infected cells, and the HIV in those cells will begin producing viruses, reestablishing high concentrations of viruses in the bloodstream, once the controlling effects of the drugs are removed.

appropriate chemicals are present. Consequently, the amount of light produced provides a report of the number of copies of the luciferase gene that are present.) The modified HIV is then used to infect cells growing in culture. The HIV-infected cells are next incubated with different drugs that the patient is taking. If there is resistant virus present, it will glow (due to the luciferase) at a higher rate than if the virus is not resistant to the drugs. Verification of resistant viruses in cell culture can occur with genotypic testing. Phenotypic testing has the advantage of directly measuring resistance under conditions similar to those seen in the body. Compared to genotypic testing it has the disadvantages that it takes longer to get test results and is more expensive. There is currently one laboratory (Monogram) that is approved to conduct phenotypic testing. There is another laboratory (Virco) that does virtual phenotype testing, based on detailed comparison of gene sequences of HIV from patients with a database of gene sequences.

Even though resistance is less likely with multiple drug treatment schemes, up to 50% of patients develop virologic failure during the first year of treatment.[17] This can occur if a patient does not adhere to the treatment, or if the patient is already infected with a resistant virus. In this case, it is sometimes possible to switch drug combinations to a set of medications to which the virus is sensitive. Often, it requires switching to new types of drugs, since viruses that are resistant to one drug in a class (e.g., one of the NNRTIs) are often resistant to many or all drugs in that class.

Prevention of HIV/AIDS

Frances Borchelt was 71 years of age when she had hip replacement surgery on August 17, 1983, at a hospital in suburban San Francisco. During the surgery, she lost a substantial amount of blood and received a transfusion of three units of blood. One of these units, it turned out, was from a man who had AIDS. By September 10, she was readmitted to the hospital with a cough and weight loss. She was initially diagnosed with hepatitis and continued to lose weight in the hospital. She was in and out of the hospital for the next several months. By early February, she had developed a painful rash that covered her entire body. Although a number of different specialists treated her, her condition did not improve. By the end of January 1985, she had suffered a bout of Pneumocystis pneumonia. Subsequently, she developed a variety of infections, including thrush, and another bout of pneumonia, and she continued to suffer from the uncontrolled rash. She was taken back to the hospital on June 10, and died that evening, less than two years after she had been infected. She was one of the first known cases of transfusion-transmitted AIDS.[1]

Since AIDS is transmitted through exchange of blood, through sexual contact or during childbirth or breastfeeding, preventive measures focus on short-circuiting each of these potential routes of infection. Preventing infection involves both technological developments and education leading to behavior modification.

PROTECTING THE BLOOD SUPPLY

In the early days of the AIDS epidemic, before the virus was identified and a blood test was available, it was estimated that the risk of acquiring HIV through a blood transfusion was as high as 1 in 440 in San Francisco during March 1985.[2] Currently, with rigorous testing and donor screening, the risk of acquiring HIV through blood transfusion in the United States is now about 1 in 2 million.[3] Methods for inactivating HIV (and other pathogens) in the blood have also been tested and implemented in some countries. An advantage of these inactivation methods is that they can target both known and unknown pathogens. For example, one approach has been to add a compound that binds to DNA or RNA. In the presence of ultraviolet light these compounds inactivate the RNA and DNA, making the viruses and other pathogens noninfectious. This treatment apparently does not affect red blood cells, which lack DNA, and have limited amounts of RNA. This inactivation method is used in Europe, and is being tested in the United States. Another approach has been to add a detergent to blood cells or platelets to disrupt the HIV envelope. This method is used in Europe as well, but its use has been discontinued in the United States out of concern for potential side effects. As methods improve for pathogen inactivation in the blood, this should further improve the safety of the blood supply from HIV as well as other pathogens.[4]

If HIV is present in a unit of blood, the risk of acquiring infection is very high. About 90% of people who get a blood transfusion from an HIV-infected donor will become HIV infected.[5] During the early 1980s, a particularly high risk group were hemophiliacs, who received clotting factors derived from the blood of hundreds of people. Heat-treatment of the clotting factors and the production of some clotting factors through genetic engineering have almost completely eliminated the risk of HIV transmission through the infusion of these medications.

Protecting the blood supply now involves both screening out donors who report high-risk behaviors, and testing of blood with both antibody-based and RNA-based screening methods to identify blood that contains HIV. Methods of treating blood to inactivate pathogens, including HIV, are also being tested.

NEEDLE EXCHANGE

Another source of blood-borne infection is contaminated needles and other medical devices that may contain blood. In developed countries this is rarely a concern in clinics, hospitals, and other medical facilities. Most of these medical devices are disposable, so reuse of needles and other equipment typically does not occur in these settings. There have been a few cases of HIV infection transmitted through a needlestick of a health-care worker, but this is rare. In contrast, in less-developed nations, particularly those in Africa, disposable needles are less common and there is still transmission of HIV through contaminated needles or other medical devices.[6]

In developed nations, one of the major areas of concern in transmission of HIV is through contaminated needles shared between intravenous drug users. Transmission of HIV through the blood is very efficient, and it does not require much blood left in a needle to transmit infection to another drug user. In addition, blood remaining in a syringe for four weeks can still harbor infectious HIV.[7] In many parts of the world, needle exchange programs, in which addicts can turn in used needles and get sterile, single use needles, have reduced the HIV transmission rate among addicts.[8] However, needle exchange is controversial in many places, and it sometimes has been difficult to find the political will to implement needle exchange programs in some areas. For example, in Russia and Eastern Europe, most HIV infections are currently being transmitted through the reuse of infected needles, yet there are few programs in place designed to reduce the frequency of HIV infection in these areas.[9] In the United States a federal law allowing government funding for needle exchange programs was not passed until 2009.[10]

BEHAVIORAL INTERVENTIONS

Getting people to change their behavior, particularly when it comes to sex and drug addiction, is a challenging proposition.

Yet behavioral changes are essential if there is going to be a reduction in the 2.5 million new cases of HIV infection that occur each year.

In terms of sexual behavior, delaying the age at first intercourse, having sex with fewer partners, using condoms during sex, and knowing the HIV status of one's partners are all effective methods of reducing HIV transmission. Educational efforts that convey this information have been successful in a number of countries. Yet a lack of knowledge of how HIV is transmitted and a lack of understanding of behaviors that can reduce transmission is still common in many of the places that have the highest risk for HIV infection.

In terms of drug use, strategies that take into account the difficulties of getting addicts to stop using drugs tend to be more effective in promoting behavior that reduces transmission of HIV. For example, needle exchanges, treatment programs (such as methadone for heroin users), counseling programs, and other related interventions tend to be more successful than campaigns that further criminalize behavior.

In general, programs aimed at preventing HIV transmission that use multiple means of communication and multiple strategies for reducing risk tend to be most successful. For example, a program intended to reduce HIV transmission among intravenous drug users in Harlem, in New York City, contained a number of elements. These included interventions such as counseling on risk reduction strategies and the distribution of pamphlets that explained how to reduce the risk of HIV infection. Other components included providing needle-collection devices with risk-reduction information, group sessions on how to avoid HIV infection, and training of pharmacists on practices they might implement to reduce the risk of users acquiring HIV. Effective interventions also included training for community-based organizations, health fairs, posters, stickers, and other sources of information.

Some programs to reduce HIV transmission between heterosexual couples in Africa have also focused on multiple education approaches to reduce HIV transmission. For example, one program in Rwanda and Zambia included education and counseling for couples, voluntary HIV testing, media dissemination about reducing the risk of HIV transmission, and community outreach programs.[11]

CONDOMS

One of the key behavioral interventions that reduces the transmission of AIDS is the use of condoms. An analysis of a large number of studies by researchers at the University of Texas Medical Branch at Galveston indicated that regular use of male condoms reduces the risk of HIV infection about 90%, similar to the reduction in pregnancy risk from consistent

Figure 5.1 **Regular use of condoms can reduce the risk of HIV transmission. (© Shutterstock)**

use of condoms.[12] Female condoms have also become more widely available in recent years. One report showed that use of a female condom every time a woman has sex reduces the risk of HIV transmission by 90%, similar to the reduction in HIV transmission with a male condom.[13]

Condoms also prevent other sexually transmitted diseases, which can also play a role in reducing the transmission of HIV through sex. For example, condoms reduce the risk of herpes simplex virus infections. Individuals with herpes infection are more likely to be infected, and infect others, with HIV, so reducing the risk of herpes infections can also reduce the risk of HIV transmission. However, condom distribution, like the distribution of other birth control, is controversial in some places. Therefore, condoms are not universally available to prevent transmission of HIV.

CIRCUMCISION

Male **circumcision** has been shown to reduce the risk of HIV transmission both from men to women, and from women to men. (Circumcision is the removal of tissue—the foreskin—from the penis.) There is a potential explanation in terms of the biology of the male genitalia. The male foreskin contains Langerhans cells, which can be infected with HIV, and which can be transmitted to a woman during intercourse. In contrast, these cells are not present on the surface of the penis in circumcised men.[14] A number of studies, dating back to 1986, suggested a reduced risk of HIV infection in men who were circumcised. The initial studies were observational, though, and could not demonstrate a causal relationship between circumcision and reduced HIV transmission. In 2005, researchers from France and South Africa reported a controlled experiment with over 3,000 initially uncircumcised men, where one group of men was circumcised, and a second group was not. The group was followed for 21 months and circumcision reduced the risk of HIV transmission by 60%.[15]

VAGINAL MICROBIOCIDES

Early studies of vaginal microbiocides involved testing traditional gels that were spermicidal, containing the chemical nonoxynol-9. The results of these studies were disappointing. In several reports there was no reduction in the incidence of HIV transmission whether or not the spermicidal gel was used. For example, in one study of almost 1,300 female sex workers in Cameroon, Africa, the rate of HIV infection was 6.7 per 100 woman years in those who used the gel, and 6.6 per 100 woman years in those who did not use a spermicidal gel.[16] In at least one other study, women were more likely to become infected after using the microbiocides than without using them.[17] In retrospect, this is not a surprising result, since the microbiocides are irritating and can induce an inflammatory response, which may increase the number of cells in the vagina that are capable of being infected with HIV.

More recently, a large-scale study tried a different approach to the prevention of HIV transmission with a vaginal microbiocide. The trial was conducted with almost 900 women in South Africa. South Africa was chosen because it has a very high rate of HIV infection and was therefore a location that was likely to provide a relatively rapid answer as to whether this approach to prevention was effective. The gel tested in this study contained tenofovir, an anti-HIV drug. Women who used the microbiocidal gel at least 80% of the time prior to and after sex had a 54% reduction in HIV infection rate, as compared with women who used a placebo.[18] Additional studies will be needed to verify this effect, but this is a potentially encouraging development in HIV prevention. A model of HIV infection in a population showed that even a gel with 40% effectiveness could, over time, substantially reduce the number of people who are infected with HIV.[19] This research also provides a starting point for additional clinical trials. For example, the use of a vaginal microbiocide containing two or more anti-HIV drugs could be tested to see if this treatment is even more effective.

POSTEXPOSURE PROPHYLAXIS

For individuals who have a clear-cut exposure to HIV, either through a needlestick or through unprotected sex with an HIV-infected individual, taking anti-HIV drugs within one to two hours after exposure is one mechanism for preventing infection. Studies in animals, starting in 1995, showed that even a single dose of an anti-retroviral drug could reduce the risk of HIV infection, if the drug was administered right after the exposure.[20] A subsequent study has shown that the use of AZT alone can reduce the risk of HIV infection following exposure about eightfold. Currently, postexposure prophylaxis consists of two or three anti-retroviral drugs taken for 28 days.[21] The idea is to prevent the virus from establishing an infection.

Similarly, some experts have recommended the use of ART, including tenofovir, another anti-HIV drug, after a high-risk sexual exposure. As yet no studies have definitively established the value of this treatment in preventing HIV transmission, although one study of this strategy found no evidence of HIV infection in 401 individuals who had a high-risk sexual or other exposure to HIV, six months after a course of antiretroviral agents.[22] A further report indicated that individuals are potentially exposed to resistant viruses, and that will need to be a factor in considering the drug or drugs to use in **postexposure prophylaxis**.[23]

PREEXPOSURE PROPHYLAXIS

There has also been the suggestion that some individuals at high risk (e.g., commercial sex workers) could benefit from taking antiretroviral drugs as a preventive measure. Several clinical trials in humans are currently in progress to test this idea. Results have been reported from one collaborative study, which was based on the efforts of a large number of scientists and others from across the globe. Approximately 2,500 gay men participated, half receiving a placebo, and half receiving a two-drug combination in a single pill. There was a reduction of

44% in the number of HIV infections in the treatment group, and that increased to 95% for those who took the drugs as prescribed. In addition, there did not appear to be increases in high-risk behavior for those participating in the study.[24]

Although this study did not show an increase in risky behavior for those individuals taking the drugs, participants did not know if they were receiving the drug or the placebo. Therefore, it may be that individuals who know they are taking the drug may end up engaging in riskier behavior. Other unresolved questions about **preexposure prophylaxis** include the extent to which uninfected people will stick to a regular routine of taking medication, whether it will increase drug resistance, and whether it is affordable and makes sense from a public health perspective, since many infected people do not currently have access to any form of treatment.[25] There is also a study being conducted to determine if a vaginal gel containing tenofovir, coupled with taking an antiretroviral medicine orally, could further reduce the rate of HIV infection in sexually active women.[26]

PREVENTING TRANSMISSION DURING PREGNANCY AND CHILDBIRTH

The risk of transmission of HIV from an infected mother to her child during pregnancy and childbirth ranges from 12–50%.[27] This range results from differences in the HIV count in the blood, the level of CD4+ cells in the woman's blood, the ability of the particular HIV strains in the mother to cross the placenta, the length of time between when the woman's water breaks and delivery, and other factors.[28]

There is some controversy about the timing of transmission of HIV from mother to infant. Some studies have suggested that HIV infection in the infant only occurs during delivery, where other studies have suggested that infection can occur prior to delivery.

Treatment of pregnant women with antiretroviral drugs is the key to preventing transmission to the infant. The use

AIDS DENIALISM AND SOUTH AFRICA

In the late 1990s, President Thabo Mbeki's government in South Africa seriously entertained the idea that HIV does not cause AIDS. The president himself questioned the safety of AZT, and individuals who denied that HIV causes AIDS were appointed to the president's advisory panel on HIV. A number of statements were made by members of the government, indicating that anti-HIV drugs were not effective, were potentially dangerous, and were part of a conspiracy to degrade Africans and interfere with the newly won democracy in South Africa. Among the results of these policies was a lack of access to anti-HIV drugs, and a lack of education about the causes and prevention of AIDS. Reports have estimated that over 300,000 South Africans have died because of these polices.[29] Starting in 2003, the South African government reversed policy, and is now working to provide education and treatment to individuals infected with HIV.[30]

of single drugs, such as AZT, was found to reduce transmission from mother to child by nearly 40%. The use of multiple drugs in standard HAART treatment likely reduces the risk of transmission from mother to child to less than 1%.[31] In addition, Cesarean section delivery further reduces the risk of infection in the infant, at least for those infants whose mothers have detectable levels of HIV in their blood during pregnancy.[32]

PREVENTING TRANSMISSION THROUGH BREAST-FEEDING

Long-term breast-feeding carries about a 12% risk of transmission of HIV to an infant.[33] Infection likely occurs from the infant ingesting infected cells in the breast milk.

Infection through this route can be prevented through the use of infant formula, rather than breast-feeding. In less-developed countries, though, the nutritional benefits from breast-feeding and the availability of clean water need to be considered in decisions about whether breast-feeding should be stopped. A recent study suggested that the risk of HIV transmission with exclusive breast-feeding for the first three months may have been no greater than the risk of HIV infection with exclusive formula feeding. On the other hand, infants who were both breast- and bottle-fed appeared to have an enhanced risk of HIV infection.[34] There are also some studies that indicate that heat treatment of breast milk (analogous to pasteurization) may inactivate the virus. This may be an option for those cases where the benefits of breast-feeding may outweigh the risk of disease transmission.[35]

6

Attempts to Develop a Vaccine for HIV/AIDS

On April 23, 1984, Margaret Heckler, the U.S. Secretary for Health and Human Services, announced the discovery of the human immunodeficiency virus. She commented that this discovery would mean that a vaccine would be ready for testing in two years and stated, "Today's discovery represents the triumph of science over a dreaded disease."[1] These statements lead to great hope that a cure and preventive vaccine would soon be available. Unfortunately, although the treatment for AIDS has improved greatly since 1984, decades later it still appears that a vaccine for AIDS is a distant prospect. The ability to cure the disease in infected people is still lacking and the current, still limited, understanding of HIV and AIDS leads to the conclusion that a cure is not likely in the near future.

Vaccination is a method for artificially stimulating an adaptive immune response against a pathogen. Since Edward Jenner's development of a smallpox vaccine in 1796, this has been the primary method for controlling viral diseases. Vaccination relies on a key property of the immune system—after initial exposure to a pathogen, the immune response to a second exposure of a pathogen is stronger, more specific, and frequently prevents symptomatic disease from developing. Therefore, when a person receives a dose of the killed or weakened virus in a vaccine, the immune system becomes educated, and can swiftly dispatch the microbial invader during the next encounter. Vaccination to prevent AIDS has several key challenges, however. One challenge is understanding what type of immune response confers protection and then developing a vaccine to produce the desired response. A second challenge is that the virus targets the very heart of the immune response, CD4+ T-cells. Therefore, another major obstacle in developing a vaccine is finding a formula that protects from infection while not harming the CD4+ T-cells. A third challenge is overcoming the clever strategies the virus has to evade an immune response. The high mutation rate of HIV, and the ability of the virus to cloak key regions of conserved viral proteins, has made it difficult to develop a vaccine that confers protection.

CHALLENGES IN DEFINING IMMUNITY

One of the major obstacles in developing an effective HIV vaccine is that it is not yet clear what type of immune response protects people from infection and the development of AIDS. Studies of HIV-infected individuals who do not develop AIDS, or individuals who have been repeatedly exposed to HIV but not infected, demonstrate that a number of genetic factors, not amenable to manipulation by a vaccine, are responsible for their resistance to the virus. Consequently, the underlying foundation for vaccine development does not yet exist, which makes many people pessimistic about the near-term development of an effective HIV vaccine.

However, there continue to be new discoveries that offer hope that the mystery surrounding immunity to HIV can be unraveled. For example, reports from scientists at the National Institutes of Health, Harvard Medical School, Rockefeller University, the University of Washington, and Columbia University described antibodies from patients that could prevent many strains of the virus from binding to and infecting cells. This was a notable finding because most antibodies against HIV only interact with a single strain of a virus, and consequently, they do not offer much protection against the wide variety of HIV strains that are circulating within a population, or even within the body of an infected person. This work could eventually lead to the development of a vaccine based on a modified HIV envelope protein that elicits broadly protective antibodies.[2]

VACCINATION WITH INACTIVATED VIRUS

For a number of viral diseases, vaccine development was almost done when the infectious agent was identified. From that discovery it was simply a matter of devising a system for growing large amounts of the pathogen, devising a way of weakening or killing the pathogen, and then vaccinating large numbers of people with the killed or weakened pathogen. Initial vaccine development for HIV used this model. Several early vaccination attempts used whole HIV, which had been inactivated through chemical treatment. These vaccines were generally tested in macaque monkeys, and the initial results were encouraging.[3] Some monkeys showed protection when challenged with a low dose of an identical strain of the virus. The protection did not extend, however, to different virus strains, or to virus that was inoculated into the genital tract. Even more discouraging, though, was the eventual realization that the protection observed in these vaccine trials was more akin to rejection of a transplant than it was to true protection from a vaccine. The virus used in these trials was grown in human cell culture. When the virus buds out of these cells it becomes decorated with human proteins. Therefore, it appears that the monkeys were primarily reacting to the human proteins on the surface of the virus, rather than to the virus itself.[4] The ultimately disappointing results from these vaccine trials set the stage for future discouraging work on HIV vaccination.

LIVE, WEAKENED HIV VACCINES

Many of the most effective vaccines for other diseases use a weakened virus. The virus can grow briefly in the body and stimulate a very strong immune response, but not cause disease. Current vaccines in this category include measles, mumps, and rubella.

Several HIV vaccines have been developed using live, weakened viruses generally created through the deletion of essential viral genes. For example, viruses with a deletion of the Nef gene have been used in vaccine studies in monkeys. These monkeys showed a significant level of protection when challenged even with unrelated viruses.

Unfortunately, this approach is not likely to lead to the development of an effective human vaccine in the near future. Baby monkeys that received the weakened virus developed an AIDS-like condition from the vaccine itself, and some adult monkeys developed AIDS-like symptoms from the vaccine as well. In addition, the weakened virus still has the ability to insert its DNA into host cells, permanently establishing an infection. There is also evidence that even human immuno-deficiency viruses with genetic deletions designed to hamper replication can undergo mutation that restores some of their virulence.[5] Although there may be ways to develop viruses that can be eliminated from the body, even the act of inserting the viral DNA into cell genomes could lead to the development of cancer.[6] Because of these problems, the use of live HIV vaccines is, at best, a distant prospect.

VACCINES THAT USE PURIFIED HIV PROTEINS

A different approach, which is considered very safe, is to use one or more HIV proteins in a vaccine. This vaccination approach has been successful for other diseases; for example, the hepatitis B vaccine uses a purified hepatitis B protein, which is churned out by genetically engineered yeast.

In HIV vaccination trials, the envelope protein and another protein, Tat, have been used. Some preliminary work with vaccination of related viruses in macaques and chimpanzees indicated that these vaccines might offer some protection against infection.[7] These vaccines were then tested in humans. Unfortunately, the results were disappointing; there was no evidence that the vaccines provided any type of protection against

HOW DO YOU PRODUCE A POTENTIAL AIDS VACCINE?

Although efforts to produce an AIDS vaccine have been unsuccessful to date, a number of different strategies have been used in the attempt to make effective HIV vaccines. The simplest vaccines are those that consist of a purified HIV protein. These vaccines are generally produced in cultured cells, such as Chinese hamster ovary cells. The cells have the HIV gene or genes added to them, and the cells are grown under conditions in which large volumes of the HIV proteins are produced. The protein or proteins are then purified, and used in the vaccine.

For vaccines that use inactivated HIV, the appropriate viral strain is used to infect a culture of human cells. After the virus has grown to large numbers, the viruses are purified from the infected cells. The viruses are then inactivated with formaldehyde and heated to 62°C (144°F). The formaldehyde cross-links proteins, thereby preventing their normal function and makes the virus unable to cause infection.

For production of live, attenuated HIV vaccines, the virus is grown in mammalian cells, typically human cells. The HIV used for this type of vaccine undergoes some genetic alteration that reduces its virulence. These viruses can be challenging to grow in large amounts, since the mutant viruses used for the vaccine often grow slowly in culture.

Canarypox, adenovirus, and other vectors have been used for some virus vaccine trials. In these cases, the virus has HIV genes inserted into the other virus. These HIV genes are inserted into the canarypox and adenovirus gene in such a way that the HIV genes are expressed once they are injected into a person. The virus is purified from the cell culture, and used for vaccination.[8]

infection from HIV.[9] It therefore seems that subunit vaccines, at least by themselves, are not going to be a solution to the problem of developing an effective anti-HIV vaccine.

VACCINES USING ANOTHER MICROBE AS A CARRIER OF HIV GENES

Based on the disappointing results with other vaccination strategies, attempts have been made to combine the best aspects of a live vaccine, with the safety of using only specific HIV proteins. These attempts use a genetically engineered virus or bacterium that contains one or more HIV genes, which in the body express HIV proteins that can stimulate an immune response. A variety of microbes have been tested for their ability to act as a vaccine vehicle, including adenovirus, rabies, canarypox, hepatitis B, influenza, poliovirus, vaccina, *Mycobacterium bovis* BCG, *Listeria*, and *Salmonella*.

This vaccination strategy has been most extensively tested using canarypox vectors. Although the efficacy was not exceptionally high, there did appear to be some protection using a canarypox virus containing HIV genes as a vaccine. In the trial, in addition to the canarypox vaccine, the study also included a separate vaccine using just the recombinant HIV gp120 protein. The vaccine showed a 26–31% reduction in the number of HIV infections in the treated group, as compared with the control group, which only received a placebo.[10] Although a high level of protection was not observed in this trial, it is hoped that these results may lead to a better understanding of immunity to HIV, which in turn, could lead to the development of more effective vaccines. Other vaccine trials have involved adenovirus vectors that express HIV proteins. One major trial using adenoviruses vectors, the Merck STEP trial, yielded results that were so disappointing that it is unlikely that much additional work will go forward with adenovirus vaccines for HIV, unless new information becomes available. In this trial, 3,000 uninfected volunteers were vaccinated on three separate occasions with either a placebo or an adenovirus that contained one HIV gene. For individuals who had preexisting high levels of antibodies to adenoviruses, it appeared that the vaccine might have increased the risk of HIV infection, just the opposite of what one would hope from a vaccine.[11]

There are approaches being taken to blunt the immune response to adenoviruses as a way to boost the effectiveness of the vaccines. However, it is clear that many challenges will have to be overcome before adenovirus vaccines are tested again for preventing HIV infection.[12]

Because of the disappointing results with AIDS vaccination to this point, several radically new strategies are being developed.

7

HIV/AIDS: Future Prospects and Concerns

Dima is an 18-year-old who lives on the streets of Odessa, Ukraine. Like many HIV-infected people in Eastern Europe, he likely acquired HIV through injecting drugs with reused, contaminated needles. Dima has had a hard life. His feet are clubbed from nerve damage from injecting a street drug called baltushka, he has lost most of his teeth, and he is homeless. Social workers located his father, who refused to take him back until he stopped taking drugs. Groups seeking to help youths like Dima run into a number of social and legal roadblocks. For example, since many of these children are not yet of legal age, social service organizations cannot provide them with anti-HIV drugs without parental consent, but the parents often cannot be located or are unwilling to be involved. Social taboos in many areas of Eastern Europe prevent the distribution of sterile needles. About a quarter of street children in Odessa are currently infected with HIV. That number is likely to grow substantially without more effective measures to curb transmission of the virus. The situation in Eastern Europe paints an alarming picture of a potential future for HIV and AIDS. In the early 1990s, HIV was almost unknown in the region. As of 2008, 1.5 million people were infected, an increase of 66% since 2001. Whether the seemingly inexorable spread of HIV in Eastern Europe or elsewhere can be stopped is one of the key questions for the future of HIV control.[1]

The challenges associated with HIV seem truly daunting. The number of people living with HIV and the number of newly infected people are growing each year. The majority of these people are in the poorest countries of Africa, who lack basic health care, and who often do not receive any treatment for HIV or other diseases. There is little prospect for an effective vaccine in the near term, and it does not seem likely that a cure for HIV infection is on the horizon. Yet, in spite of much discouraging results, there have been success stories related to HIV and AIDS that offer hope.

THE CHALLENGE OF PROVIDING TREATMENT TO ALL WHO NEED IT

In developed nations, most people who need treatment for HIV are able to get it. However, in countries where the need is greatest, particularly in Africa, frequently only half or fewer of the patients who need treatment can get it. A number of organizations, such as the Bill and Melinda Gates Foundation, provided substantial financial support to provide treatment in less developed nations. However, the need is so great that there still is not sufficient funding to provide treatment for all people who need it. The cost for a year of anti-HIV drug treatment in less developed countries is currently approximately $200 (through the Clinton HIV/AIDS Initiative).[2] Although this seems like a relatively small amount of money, the average yearly amount spent for health care in many of these countries is often less than $100.[3] Consequently, the cost of drugs to treat HIV is a substantial burden. International donors have worked to fill these funding gaps, but many people in less-developed countries are still not receiving adequate treatment. The United Nations estimated in 2009 that only about one-third of those eligible for treatment with antiretroviral drugs are receiving the treatment they need.[4]

With inadequate treatment of many people, the likelihood is that HIV transmission will continue at a high rate and millions of people will continue to die from HIV infection. One option is to spend available funds more quickly, in hopes of reducing the number of people who are infected now and into the future, reducing the total amount of money needed in the end.[5]

THE CHALLENGE OF DRUG RESISTANCE

The high mutation rate of HIV poses a major problem for treating people who are infected. Since the virus becomes a permanent resident of the body following infection, treatment needs to continue for a lifetime. Even with good adherence to an effective treatment regime, up to 50% of patients lose control of their HIV infection during the first year, and require new treatment options. This is likely to pose a continuing challenge in effectively treating patients with HIV infections.

Any letup of treatment allows the virus to replicate again and makes the likelihood of developing resistance even greater. In some cases, the drugs a person takes have different half-lives, so there may be an effective concentration of only one or two drugs for a period of time each day. This can select for viruses that are resistant to one of the drugs. Over time, if adherence to the drug regime is intermittent, viruses that are resistant to multiple drugs can develop, requiring new drug choices, some of which may have more serious side effects. Eventually a situation could develop where a person may have few choices left for drug treatment.

THE LONG-TERM EFFECTS OF ANTI-HIV TREATMENT

Highly active antiretroviral treatment (HAART) has been available since 1996. The various classes of anti-HIV drugs have a number of serious side effects, and it is not certain what the effects of long-term drug treatment will be. In many cases there is conflicting information, but some analysis has indicated an increased risk of cardiovascular disease following the use of some antiretroviral agents.[6] There is also the potential for liver damage and kidney damage following long-term use of at least some antiretrovirals. Other chronic effects of treatment include changes in fat distribution (lipodystrophy) that have been associated with increased risk of heart attack, and a loss of sensation in the extremities.[7] Considering that HAART has only been widely available for about 15 years, the extent to which the effects of treatment will be manageable over three or four decades is still unknown.

THE POTENTIAL THAT TREATMENT CAN LEAD TO GREATER TRANSMISSION OVER TIME

HAART is important for improving the lives of patients, and reducing the risk of death. However, it is possible that over the long course of the illness more people will become infected with HIV than if treatment were not available. This could occur, for example, if infected people are healthy for longer periods of time, and consequently have more sexual partners who subsequently get infected.[8] Therefore, education has a key role in modifying people's behavior to reduce the risk of HIV infection.

CHALLENGES IN DEVELOPED COUNTRIES

The rate of new HIV infections is still disturbingly high. In the United States during the first decade of the 21st century, the number of new infections each year remained stubbornly around 50,000. With the development of HAART some complacency has taken root, and the behavioral modifications that some individuals had adopted to prevent transmission of HIV has waned. Consequently, HIV infection continues to be a threat, and continued educational programs are required.

CHALLENGES IN DEVELOPING COUNTRIES

The challenges surrounding HIV infection in developing countries are even more severe than those in developed countries. The key challenges are reducing the transmission of HIV to infants and young children, providing treatment to all infected individuals, and reducing the effect of HIV/AIDS on orphans and others who are not infected, but are directly affected by AIDS in countries lacking resources.[9]

The knowledge is available to prevent the transmission of HIV from mother to child in almost all cases, but a lack of funding and a lack of access to medical care mean many infants are currently born HIV-infected. These problems are compounded when conflict, corruption, lack of funding, and other factors need to be addressed before appropriate care can be provided.

What is needed is increased funding, probably about double the current funding levels. This money is needed to support effective prevention programs, to provide treatment to people who need it, to allow for the development of more clinics and hospitals so more people have access to medical care, and to reduce illiteracy so that education programs can be more effective.

FUTURE PROSPECTS FOR CURING HIV INFECTION

In scientific research, it is difficult to know where the next major breakthrough might come from. One key is to provide sufficient support for research so that many possible strategies can be explored. This idea certainly applies to curing HIV infection. Currently, this appears to be an intractable problem with little hope for resolution in the near term. Yet, as new aspects of viral biology and cell biology are uncovered, the prospects for something as distant as a cure for HIV infection begin to come into focus.

One example of how new insights into biology might someday lead to a cure comes from an understanding of microRNAs. Originating in basic studies of the biology of a tiny worm that eats bacteria, scientists learned these small RNA molecules play an important role in cells, including fighting some viral infections. The microRNAs are produced naturally by infected cells. These small RNAs serve as a guide for identifying and destroying RNAs from viruses, such as HIV. Many viruses have

developed countermeasures to overcome the effects of micro-
RNAs. For example, scientists from France and the United
States demonstrated that HIV lowers the expression of micro-
RNAs that would otherwise help control infection.[10]

Following on this basic advance in the scientific understanding of the role microRNAs play in immunity, there have been
attempts to develop treatments for people who are infected with
HIV. The goal is to be able to wean these individuals off anti-
HIV drugs. Eventually, methods may be developed that could
harness this strategy to genetically modify our cells to make
them resistant to HIV infection. For example, basic research in
cell culture has shown that the production of microRNAs that
prevent the cells from making CCR5 or CXCR4 co-receptors
makes the cells resistant to HIV infection.[11] Related research
could lead to the development of microRNAs that directly target HIV and prevent the virus from infecting or replicating in
cells. There is evidence, for example, that naturally occurring
microRNAs can reduce HIV replication in cells. Enhancing the
production of these microRNAs could allow for effective control of the virus by fully preventing HIV replication.[12]

An idea related to microRNAs is called antisense RNA.
In this case a longer RNA is produced in a cell, which is
the complementary RNA strand to the target RNA. Likely
through a process that involves cleaving the longer RNA to
microRNAs, the target RNA is destroyed, and the expression
of that gene is eliminated. This strategy was attempted in a
small clinical trial to test the safety of this approach in treating
HIV infection.[13]

In this trial, five patients had some of their CD4+ T-cells
removed. These cells were then infected with an HIV that
lacked all the viral genes, and contained only the ends of the
HIV genome (the long terminal repeats) and an antisense
partial copy of the HIV envelope gene. The cells were grown
in culture to expand the cell population, and then transfused
back into the patients. The intention was that these defective

viruses could infect HIV-infected cells and prevent the viruses from replicating, interfering with the production of new HIV. Four out of five of the patients saw some improvement in their immune function following treatment, suggesting some hope for this approach to treating HIV infection.[14]

Another example of a basic scientific finding that might have importance in curing HIV infection is an understanding of what keeps a virus (like HIV) inert once it is in a cell. The ability to activate the virus could allow infected cells to be effectively targeted and eliminated from the body. This could allow for the elimination of infected cells, and potentially the elimination of HIV. There is an increasing understanding of what specific mechanisms allow HIV to remain hidden in a cell. Additional research may unlock some of the clues that would allow for unmasking these HIV-infected cells and expose them to an effective immune response that would purge the virus from the body.[15]

FUTURE PROSPECTS FOR VACCINATION AND OTHER MEASURES THAT COULD PREVENT HIV INFECTION

It appears that the road toward developing an effective vaccine will be a long one. A lack of understanding of what constitutes immunity to HIV, a realization that some anti-HIV immune responses actually facilitate virus replication, and the difficulty of purging a pathogen that lurks in our own genomes are all daunting challenges.

It is clear that traditional vaccination strategies involving inactivated viruses, weakened viruses, or individual proteins from the virus are unlikely to lead to protective immunity. Therefore, a better understanding of immunity in general, and immunity to HIV in particular, will be a key to developing an effective vaccine. In addition, developing a better understanding of how HIV initially establishes infection will be a key to efforts to prevent disease transmission.

USING HIV TO TREAT DISEASE

HIV is one of the most serious and intractable pathogens that we face today, yet in an odd twist, some of the same properties that make the virus so potent as an infectious agent have the potential to work for the benefit of those suffering from certain genetic diseases.

Adrenoleukodystrophy (ALD), a genetic disease afflicting males almost exclusively, affects about 1 in 20,000 boys. The disease results from a disorder in fat metabolism because of a mutation in the ABCD1 gene that is involved in transporting fats within cells. ALD leads to a progressive loss of movement and speech starting at around age six. Eventually it causes paralysis and blindness, and most victims die before their teenage years. Although it is uncommon, the disease became well-known following the movie *Lorenzo's Oil*. Although touted as a treatment, the oil is not very effective once symptoms develop. Bone marrow transplants have been successful in some patients, but transplants are risky, since patients must take immune-suppressing drugs for life. In addition, it is not always possible to find a matching bone marrow donor for a patient.

In an effort to develop a more general strategy for treating or preventing ALD, scientists from France and the United States used gene therapy as a treatment. As a starting point the scientists tested their treatment on two seven-year-old

There is now a clearer understanding of how some individuals develop antibodies that offer protection against infection, and this should help contribute to the development of an effective vaccine. Innovative approaches to vaccination are constantly being developed, and these may someday contribute to preventing HIV transmission. For example, as noted above, a method of reducing CXCR4 and CCR5 expression has been boys. The boys had no matching bone marrow donor and had begun showing symptoms of ALD, so their prognosis was poor.

The gene therapy was intended to insert a functional copy of the gene in bone marrow stem cells of these young patients. A HIV-based, disabled virus was used to deliver the gene to bone marrow stem cells that were isolated from the boys. A disabled virus was used because it had the ability to permanently infect stem cells (unlike other viruses) but could not cause AIDS because it lacked essential viral genes.

Once the bone marrow stem cells were isolated, and infected with the virus, the boys were treated with chemotherapy to destroy their bone marrow. The HIV-transformed cells with the functional ABCD1 gene were then infused in the boys. In both cases the genetically engineered cells "took" and reconstituted the bone marrow. The boys were followed for two and a half years, and their disease did not progress any further. Since the cells for the bone marrow transplant came from the boys themselves, there was no need to take immune-suppressing drugs to prevent the cells from being rejected. This small-scale experiment shows the potential for HIV as an agent of gene therapy. The fact that the virus can infect a variety of blood cells, including stem cells, makes it both a potent foe in causing disease, and a potential ally in treating genetic disease.[16]

developed and tested in cells in culture. Although many technical hurdles remain, a strategy like this may provide gene-based protection against HIV.[17]

As another example of an encouraging development, there is a report of a person infected with HIV who appears to have been cured. This person had leukemia in addition to AIDS and received a bone marrow transplant from a person who had

a CCR5 mutation. The transplant involved eliminating all of
the patient's bone marrow cells and many cells of the immune
system. After the transplant with HIV-resistant bone marrow,
the person did not have any evidence of HIV infection for the
two-year follow-up reported in the study. This case shows the
potential for gene therapy to eliminate HIV infection, although
this specific treatment would not be possible for widespread
use, since it requires a matching donor with a CCR5 mutation.[18]

Other work, including improved immune boosters (**adjuvants**) in vaccines, the development of vaccine strategies
that use DNA containing HIV genes, and other innovative
approaches involving nanotechnology,[19] may open the door to
a future with a vaccine that will prevent infection.

Chapter 1

1. R. White, *My Own Story* (New York: Signet, 1992).
2. World Health Organization, "The Top 10 Leading Causes of Death (2004)," http://www.who.int/mediacentre/factsheets/fs310/en/index.html (accessed August 13, 2010).
3. B. Keele et al., "Chimpanzee Reservoirs of Pandemic and Nonpandemic HIV-1," *Science* 313 (2006): 523–526.
4. J. Cohen, "Island Monkeys Give Clues to Origins of HIV's Ancestor," *ScienceNOW* (2010), http://news.sciencemag.org/sciencenow/2010/07/island-monkeys-give-clues-to-ori.html (accessed August 15, 2010).
5. E. Bailes et al., "Hybrid Origin of SIV in Chimpanzees," *Science* 300 (2003): 1713.
6. J. Heeney, A. Dalgleish, and R. Weiss, "Origins of HIV and the Evolution of Resistance to AIDS," *Science* 313 (2006): 462–466.
7. P. Sax, C. Cohen, and D. Kuritzkes, *HIV Essentials*, 3d ed. (Sudbury, Mass.: Jones and Bartlett, 2010).
8. L. Barat et al., "Bacterial Infections Are the Most Common Cause of Fever in HIV-infected Patients Admitted to a Municipal Hospital," *International Conference on AIDS* 8 (1992): B229, http://gateway.nlm.nih.gov/MeetingAbstracts/ma?f=102199270.html (accessed August 14, 2010).
9. O. Tawfik, C. Papasian, A. Dixon, and L. Potter, "*Saccharomyces cerevisiae* Pneumonia in a Patient with Acquired Immune Deficiency Syndrome," *Journal of Clinical Microbiology* 27 (1989): 1689–1691.
10. M. Ghafouri, S. Amini, K. Khalili, and B. Sawaya, "HIV-1 Associated Dementia: Symptoms and Causes," *Retrovirology* 3 (2006): 28.
11. R. Ellis, P. Calero, and M. Stockin, "HIV Infection and the Central Nervous System: A Primer," *Neuropsychological Review* 19 (2009): 144–151.
12. World Health Organization, "The Global Burden of Disease: 2004 Update," http://www.who.int/healthinfo/global_burden_disease/2004_report_update/en/index.html (accessed August 13, 2010).
13. G. Bohnsack and H. Brehmer, *Auftrag: Irreführung: Wie die Stasi Politik im Westen machte.* (Hamburg, Germany: Carlsen, 1992).
14. T. Boghardt, "Operation INFEKTION: Soviet Bloc Intelligence and Its AIDS Disinformation Campaign," *Studies in Intelligence* 53 (2009): 1–24, https://www.cia.gov/library/center-for-the-study-of-intelligence/csi-publications/csi-studies/studies/vol53no4/pdf/U-%20Boghardt-AIDS-Made%20in%20the%20USA-17Dec.pdf (accessed August 9, 2010).
15. L. Bogart, S. Kalichman, and L. Simbayi, "Endorsement of a Genocidal HIV Conspiracy as a Barrier to HIV Testing in South Africa," *Journal of Acquired Immune Deficiency Syndromes* 49 (2008): 115–116.
16. M. McKenna, C. Michaud, C. Murray, and J. Marks, "Assessing the Burden of Disease in the United States Using Disability-Adjusted Life Years," *American Journal of Preventive Medicine* 28 (2005): 415–423.
17. P. Duesberg, *Inventing the AIDS Virus* (Washington, D.C.: Regnery, 2006).
18. National Institute of Allergy and Infectious Disease, *The Evidence that HIV Causes AIDS*, http://www.niaid.nih.gov/topics/HIVAIDS/Understanding/how HIVCausesAIDS/Pages/HIVcausesAIDS.aspx (accessed on August 14, 2010).
19. S.H. Vermund, D. Hoover, and K. Chen, "CD4+ Counts in Seronegative Homosexual Men: The Multicenter AIDS Cohort Study," *The New England Journal of Medicine* 328 (1993): 442.
20. D. C. Des Jarlais et al., "CD4 Lymphocytopenia among Injecting Drug Users in New York City," *Journal of Acquired Immune Deficiency Syndrome* 6 (1993): 820–822.
21. M. Schechter et al., "HIV-1 and the Etiology of AIDS," *The Lancet* 341 (1993): 658–659.

22. National Institute of Allergy and Infectious Disease, "The Evidence that HIV causes AIDS."

23. C. Sabin et al., "Comparison of Immunodeficiency and AIDS Defining Conditions in HIV Negative and HIV Positive Men with Hemophilia A," *British Medical Journal* 312 (1996): 207–210.

24. G. Jersey et al., "Effect of Low- and Intermediate-purity Clotting Factor Therapy on Progression of Human Immunodeficiency Virus Infection in Congenital Clotting Disorders: Transfusion Safety Study Group," *Blood* 84 (1994): 1666–1671.

25. G. White, "Hemophilia: An Amazing 35-Year Journey from the Depths of HIV to the Threshold of Cure," *Transactions of the American Clinical and Climatological Association* 121 (2010): 61–75.

26. A. Mycroft et al., "AIDS Across Europe, 1994–98: the EuroSIDA Study," *The Lancet* 356 (2000): 291–296.

27. S. Hammer et al. for the Aids Clinical Trials Group 320 Study Team, "A Controlled Trial of Two Nucleoside Analogues Plus Indinavir in Persons with Human Immunodeficiency Virus Infection and CD4 Cell Counts of 200 per Cubic Millimeter or Less," *The New England Journal of Medicine* 337 (1997): 725–733.

28. S. O'Brien and J. Goedert, "HIV Causes AIDS: Koch's Postulates Fulfilled," *Current Opinion in Immunology* 8 (1996): 613–618.

29. C. A. Stoddart et al., "Validation of the SCID-hu Thy/Liv Mouse Model with Four Classes of Licensed Antiretrovirals," *PLoS ONE* 2 (2007): e655.

Chapter 2

1. R. Shilts, *And the Band Played On. Politics, People, and the AIDS Epidemic.* 20th ed. (New York: St. Martin's Griffin, 1988).

2. Centers for Disease Control, "Pneumocystis pneumonia—Los Angeles," *Morbidity and Mortality Weekly Report* 30 (1981): 250–252.

3. A. Nahmias et al., "Evidence for Human Infection with an HTLVIII/LAV-like Virus in Central Africa, 1959," *The Lancet* 31 (1986): 1279–1280.

4. T. Zhu et al., "An African HIV-1 Sequence from 1959 and Implications for the Origin of the Epidemic," *Nature* 391 (1998): 594–597.

5. M. Worobey et al., "Direct Evidence of Extensive Diversity of HIV-1 in Kinshasa by 1960," *Nature* 455 (2008): 661–664.

6. J. Cohen, "Island Monkeys Give Clues to Origins of HIV's Ancestor." M. Worobey et al., "Island Biogeography Reveals the Deep History of SIV," *Science* 329 (2010): 148.

7. J. Levy, *HIV and the Pathogenesis of AIDS.* 3d ed. (Washington, D.C.: American Society for Microbiology Press, 2007), 23.

8. P. Sharp and B. Hahn, "The Evolution of HIV-1 and the Origin of AIDS," *Philosophical Transactions of the Royal Society B* 365 (2010): 2487–2494.

9. E. Drucker, P. Alcabes, and, P. Marx, "The Injection Century: Massive Unsterile Injections and the Emergence of Human Pathogens," *The Lancet* 358 (2001): 1989–1992.

10. M. T. Gilbert et al., "The Emergence of HIV/AIDS in the Americas and Beyond," *Proceedings of the National Academy of Sciences, USA* 104 (2007): 18566–18570.

11. The Nobel Assembly at Karolinska Institute, "Physiology or Medicine 1975," press release, Nobelprize.org, http://nobelprize.org/nobel_prizes/medicine/laureates/1975/press.html (accessed September 20, 2010).

12. R. Gallo, "A Reflection on HIV/AIDS Research after 25 Years," *Retrovirology* 3 (2006): 72.

13. Ibid.

14. F. Barré-Sinoussi et al., "Isolation of a T-lymphotropic Retrovirus from a Patient at Risk for Acquired Immune Deficiency Syndrome (AIDS)," *Science* 220 (1983): 868–871.

15. L. Montagnier et al., "A New Human T-lymphotrophic Retrovirus:

Characterization and Possible Role in Lymphadenopathy and Acquired Immune Deficiency Syndromes," in *Human T-cell Leukemia/Lymphoma Virus* (Cold Spring Harbor, N.Y.: Cold Spring Harbor Laboratory, 1984), 363–379; L. Montagnier et al., "Adaptation of Lymphadenopathy Associated Virus (LAV) to Replication in EBV-transformed B Lymphoblastoid Cell Lines," *Science* 225 (1984): 63–66; J. Levy et al., "Isolation of Lymphocytopathic Retroviruses from San Francisco Patients with AIDS," *Science* 225 (1984): 840–842; R. Gallo et al., "Frequent Detection and Isolation of Cytopathic Retroviruses (HTLV-III) from Patients with AIDS and At Risk for AIDS," *Science* 224 (1984): 500–503; M. Popovic, M. Sarngadharan, E. Read, and R. Gallo, "Detection, Isolation, and Continuous Production of Cytopathic Retroviruses (HTLV-III) from Patients with AIDS and Pre-AIDS," *Science* 224 (1984): 497–500.

16. J. Levy, *HIV and the Pathogenesis of AIDS.*

17. P. Lusso, "HIV and the Chemokine System: 10 Years Later," *EMBO Journal* 25 (2006): 447–456.

18. The Nobel Assembly at Karolinska Institute, "Physiology or Medicine 1975."

19. J. Levy, *HIV and the Pathogenesis of AIDS*, 13.

20. S. Belshaw et al., "Long-term Reinfection of the Human Genome by Endogenous Retroviruses," *Proceedings of the National Academy of Sciences, USA* 101 (2004): 4894–4899.

21. A. Muir, A. Lever, and A. Moffett, "Expression and Functions of Human Endogenous Retroviruses in the Placenta: an update," *Placenta* Supplement A (2004): S16–S25.

22. J. Heeney, A. Dalgleish, and R. Weiss, "Origins of HIV and the Evolution of Resistance to AIDS."

23. E. Hooper, *The River: A Journey to the Source of HIV and AIDS* (Boston, Mass.: Little, Brown and Co., 1999); E. Hooper, "AIDS and the Polio Vaccine," *London Review of Books* 25 (2003): 22–23.

24. P. Osterrieth, "Oral Polio Vaccine: Fact Versus Fiction," *Vaccine* 22 (2004): 1831–1835.

25. S. Plotkin, "Chimpanzees and Journalists," *Vaccine* 22 (2004): 1829–1830.

26. P. Blancou et al., "Polio Vaccine Samples Not Linked to AIDS," *Nature* 410 (2001): 1045–1046; N. Berry et al., "Vaccine Safety: Analysis of Oral Polio Vaccine CHAT Stocks," *Nature* 410 (2001): 1046–1047.

27. M. Worobey et al., "Origin of AIDS: Contaminated Polio Vaccine Theory Refuted," *Nature* 428 (2004): 820.

28. A. S. Jegede, "What Led to the Nigerian Boycott of the Polio Vaccination Campaign?" *PLoS Med* 4 (2007): e73.

29. The Nobel Assembly at Karolinska Institute, "The Discoveries of Human Papilloma Viruses that Cause Cervical Cancer and of Human Immunodeficiency Virus," http://nobelprize.org/nobel_prizes/medicine/laureates/2008/adv.pdf (accessed on September 13, 2010).

30. A. Vahlen, "A Historical Reflection on the Discovery of Human Retroviruses," *Retrovirology* 6 (2009): 40.

31. X. Wu et al., "Rational Design of Envelope Identifies Broadly Neutralizing Human Monoclonal Antibodies to HIV-1," *Science* 329 (2010): 856–861; T. Zhou et al., "Structural Basis for Broad and Potent Neutralization of HIV-1 by Antibody VRCO1," *Science* 329 (2010): 811–817.

32. K. Abdoo et al. "Effectiveness and Safety of Tenofovir Gel, an Antiretroviral Microbiocide, for the Prevention of HIV Infection in Women," *Science* 329 (2010): 1168–1174.

33. R. Grant et al., "Preexposure Chemoprophylaxis for HIV Prevention in Men Who Have Sex with Men," *New England Journal of Medicine* (November 23, 2010): 10.1056/NEJMoa1011205.

34. J. Cohen, "Money Woes Cast Shadow over HIV/AIDS, but Ray of Light in South Africa," *Science* 329 (2010): 500–501.

Chapter 3

1. "An AIDS Orphan's Story," *BBC World News*, November 27, 2002, http://news.bbc.co.uk/2/hi/africa/2511829.stm (accessed September 6, 2010).

2. World AIDS Orphans Day, "The Orphans Crisis: The Facts," http://www.worldaidsorphans.org/section/the_orphans_crisis/the_facts (accessed October 2, 2010).

3. UNAIDS/WHO Working Group on Global HIV/AIDS and STI Surveillance, "Epidemiological Fact Sheet on HIV and AIDS: Core Data on Epidemiology and Response, United States of America," http://www.unaids.org/en/Knowledge Centre/HIVData/Epidemiology/epifactsheets.asp (accessed November 13, 2010).

4. UNAIDS/WHO Working Group on Global HIV/AIDS and STI Surveillance, "Epidemiological Fact Sheet on HIV and AIDS: Core Data on Epidemiology and Response, South Africa," http://www.unaids.org/en/KnowledgeCentre/HIVData/Epidemiology/epifactsheets.asp (accessed November 13, 2010).

5. E. Freed, "HIV-1 Gag Proteins: Diverse Functions in the Virus Life Cycle," *Virology* 251 (1998): 1–15.

6. J. Levy, *HIV and the Pathogenesis of AIDS.*

7. C. Liang and M. Wainberg, "The Role of Tat in HIV-1 Replication: an Activator and/or a Suppressor?" *AIDS Review* 4 (2002): 41–49.

8. H. Xiao et al., "Selective CXCR4 Antagonism by Tat: Implications for In Vivo Expansion of Coreceptor Use by HIV-1," *Proceedings of the National Academy of Sciences, USA* 97 (2000): 11466–11471.

9. A. Joseph, M. Kumar, and D. Mitra, "Nef: 'Necessary and Enforcing Factor' in HIV Infection," *Current HIV Research* 3 (2005): 87–94.

10. J. Levy, *HIV and the Pathogenesis of AIDS*, 88.

11. Ibid.

12. J. Homsy, M. Meyer, and J. Levy, "Serum Enhancement of Human Immunodeficiency Virus (HIV) Infection Correlates with Disease in HIV-Infected Individuals," *Journal of Virology* 64 (1990): 1437–1440.

13. D. Douek, M. Roederer, and R. Koup, "Emerging Concepts in the Immunopathogenesis of AIDS."

14. J. Levy, *HIV and the Pathogenesis of AIDS*, 88.

15. Ibid.

16. D. Douek, M. Roederer, and R. Koup, "Emerging Concepts in the Immunopathogenesis of AIDS," *Annual Review of Medicine* 60 (2009): 471–484.

17. J. Levy, *HIV and the Pathogenesis of AIDS*, 88.

18. A. Joseph, M. Kumar, and D. Mitra, "Nef: 'Necessary and Enforcing Factor' in HIV Infection."

19. T. Hatziioannou et al., "A Macaque Model of HIV-1 Infection," *Proceedings of the National Academy of Sciences USA* 106 (2009): 4425–4429.

20. C. A. Stoddart et al., "Validation of the SCID-hu Thy/Liv Mouse Model with Four Classes of Licensed Antiretrovirals."

21. J. Levy, *HIV and the Pathogenesis of AIDS*, 88.

22. J. Fellay, K.V. Shianna, A. Telenti, D. B. Goldstein, "Host Genetics and HIV-1: The Final Phase?" *PLoS Pathogens* 6 (2010): e1001033.

23. T. Miura et al., "Genetic Characterization of Human Immunodeficiency Virus Type 1 in Elite Controllers: Lack of Gross Genetic Defects or Common Amino Acid Changes," *Journal of Virology* 82 (2008): 8422–8430.

24. J. Fellay, K.V. Shianna, A. Telenti, D. B. Goldstein, "Host Genetics and HIV-1: The Final Phase?"

25. D. van Manen et al., "The Effect of *Trim5* Polymorphisms on the Clinical Course of HIV-1 Infection," *PLoS Pathogens* 4 (2008): e18.

26. P. An et al., "Regulatory Polymorphisms in the Cyclophilin A Gene, PPIA,

Accelerate Progression to AIDS," *PLoS Pathogens* 3(2007): e88.

27. J. Blankson, "Effector Mechanisms in HIV-1 Infected Elite Controllers: Highly Active Immune Responses?" *Antiviral Research* 85 (2010) 295–302.

Chapter 4

1. H. Grossman, "AIDS at 25: A Quarter Century of Medical Miracles," *Medscape General Medicine* 8 (2006): 57.
2. P. Sax, C. Cohen, and D. Kuritzkes, *HIV Essentials.*
3. D. Gallo et al., "Evaluation of a System Using Oral Mucosal Transudate for HIV-1 Antibody Screening and Confirmatory Testing," *Journal of the American Medical Association* 277 (1997): 254–258.
4. Busch et al., "Current and Emerging Infectious Risks of Blood Transfusions," *Journal of the American Medical Association* 289 (2003): 959–962.
5. National Institutes of Health, "DHHS Panel on Antiretroviral Guidelines for Adults and Adolescents Guidelines for the Use of Antiretroviral Agents in HIV-1-Infected Adults and Adolescents, 2009," http://aidsinfo.nih.gov/content files/AdultandAdolescentGL.pdf (accessed September 3, 2010).
6. K. Brinkman, H. ter Hofstede, D. Burger, J. Smeitink, and P. Koopmans, "Adverse Effects of Reverse Transcriptase Inhibitors: Mitochondrial Toxicity as Common Pathway," *AIDS* 12 (1998): 1735–1744.
7. T. Cihlar and A. Ray, "Nucleoside and Nucleotide HIV Reverse Transcriptase Inhibitors: 25 Years after Zidovudine," *Antiviral Research* 85 (2010): 39–58.
8. M.P. de Béthune, "Non-nucleoside Reverse Transcriptase Inhibitors (NNRTIs), Their Discovery, Development, and Use in the Treatment of HIV-1 Infection: A Review of the Last 20 Years (1989–2009)," *Antiviral Research* 85 (2010): 75–90.
9. R. Ellis et al. and the CHARTER Group, "HIV Protease Inhibitors and Risk of

Peripheral Neuropathy," *Annals of Neurology* 64 (2008): 566–572.

10. J. Tilton and R. Doms, "Entry Inhibitors in the Treatment of HIV-1 Infection," *Antiviral Research* 85 (2010): 91–100.
11. Ibid.
12. D. McColl and X. Chen, "Strand Transfer Inhibitors of HIV-1 Integrase: Bringing in a New Era of Antiretroviral Therapy," *Antiviral Research* 85 (2010): 101–118.
13. J. Ioannidis et al., "Early or Deferred Zidovudine Therapy in HIV-Infected Patients without an AIDS-Defining Illness. A Meta-Analysis," *Annals of Internal Medicine* 122 (1995): 857–866; M. Seligmann et al., "Concorde: MRC/ANRS Randomized Double-blind Controlled Trial of Immediate and Deferred Zidovudine in Symptom-free HIV Infection," *Lancet* 343 (1994): 871–881.
14. R. De Boer, R. Ribeiro, and A. Perelson, "Current Estimates for HIV-1 Production Imply Rapid Viral Clearance in Lymphoid Tissues," *PLoS Computational Biology* 6 (9): e1000906.
15. P. Sax, C. Cohen, and D. Kuritzkes, *HIV Essentials.*
16. National Institutes of Health, "Guidelines for the Use of Antiretroviral Agents in HIV-1-Infected Adults and Adolescents: Tables," http://aidsinfo.nih.gov/contentfiles/AA_Tables.pdf (accessed May 3, 2010).
17. R. Grant et al., "Accuracy of the TRUGENE HIV-1 Genotyping Kit," *Journal of Clinical Microbiology* 41 (2003): 1586–1593.

Chapter 5

1. R. Shilts, *And the Band Played On. Politics, People, and the AIDS Epidemic.*
2. Ibid.
3. S. Stramer et al., "Detection of HIV-1 and HCV Infections among Antibody-Negative Blood Donors by Nucleic Acid–Amplification Testing," *New England Journal of Medicine* 351 (2004): 760–768.
4. J. Allain et al., "Protecting the Blood Supply from Emerging Pathogens: the Role of Pathogen Inactivation,"

Transfusion Medicine Review 19 (2005): 110–126.

5. J. Levy, *HIV and the Pathogenesis of AIDS*, 88.

6. S. Reid and A. A. Van Niekerk, "Injection Risks and HIV Transmission in the Republic of South Africa," *International Journal of Sexually Transmitted Diseases and AIDS* 20 (2009): 816–819; S. Reid, "Non-vertical HIV Transmission to Children in Sub-Saharan Africa," *International Journal of Sexually Transmitted Diseases and AIDS*. 20 (2009): 820–827.

7. A. Nadia, C. Stephens, B. Griffith, and R. Heimer, "Survival of HIV-1 in Syringes," *Journal of Acquired Immune Deficiency Syndromes & Human Retrovirology* 20 (1999): 73–80.

8. D. Gibson, N. Flynn, and D. Perales, "Effectiveness of Syringe Exchange Programs in Reducing HIV Risk Behavior and HIV Seroconversion among Injecting Drug Users," *AIDS* 15 (2001): 1329–1341.

9. J. Cohen, "Late for the Epidemic: HIV/AIDS in Europe," *Science* 329 (2010): 160–164; J. Cohen, "HIV Moves in on Homeless Youth," *Science* 329 (2010): 170–171.

10. Centers for Disease Control and Prevention, "Department of Health and Human Services Implementation Guidance for Syringe Services Programs July 2010," http://www.cdc.gov/hiv/resources/guidelines/PDF/SSP-guidanceacc.pdf (accessed November 14, 2010).

11. T. Coates, L. Richter, and C. Caceres, "Behavioural Strategies to Reduce HIV Transmission: How to Make Them Work Better," *Lancet* 372 (2008): 669–684.

12. K. Davis and S. Weller, "The Effectiveness of Condoms in Reducing Heterosexual Transmission of HIV," *Family Planning Perspectives* 31(1999): 272–279.

13. B. Shane et al., "Female Condom: A Powerful Tool for Protection," https://www.unfpa.org/webdav/site/global/shared/documents/publications/2006/female_condom.pdf (accessed September 12, 2010).

14. R. Szabo and R. Short, "How Does Male Circumcision Protect against HIV Infection?" *British Medical Journal* 320 (2000): 1592–1594.

15. B. Auvert et al., "Randomized, Controlled Intervention Trial of Male Circumcision for Reduction of HIV Infection Risk: The ANRS 1265 Trial," *PLoS Medicine* 2 (2005): e298.

16. R. Roddy et al., "A Controlled Trial of Nonoxynol 9 Film to Reduce Male-to-Female Transmission of Sexually Transmitted Diseases," *New England Journal of Medicine* 339 (1998): 504–510.

17. J. Kreiss et al., "Efficacy of Nonoxynol 9 Contraceptive Sponge Use in Preventing Heterosexual Acquisition of HIV in Nairobi Prostitutes," *Journal of the American Medical Association* 268 (1992): 477–482.

18. A. Karim et al., "Effectiveness and Safety of Tenofovir Gel, an Antiretroviral Microbiocide, for the Prevention of HIV Infection in Women," *Science* 329 (2010): 1168–1174.

19. C. Watts and P. Vickerman, "The Impact of Microbiocides on HIV and STD Transmission: Model Projections," *AIDS* 15 (2001): S43–S44.

20. Centers for Disease Control and Prevention, "Case-Control Study of HIV Seroconversion in Health-Care Workers After Percutaneous Exposure to HIV-Infected Blood–France, United Kingdom, and United States, January 1988–August 1994," *Morbidity and Mortality Weekly Report* 44: 929–933.

21. Centers for Disease Control and Prevention, "Notice to Readers Update: Provisional Public Health Service Recommendations For Chemoprophylaxis After Occupational Exposure to HIV," *Morbidity and Mortality Weekly Report* 45 (1996): 468–472.

22. J. Kahn et al., "Feasibility of Postexposure Prophylaxis (PEP) against Human

Immunodeficiency Virus Infection after Sexual or Injection Drug Use Exposure: The San Francisco PEP Study," *Journal of Infectious Diseases* 183 (2001): 707–714.

23. M. Roland et al., "Postexposure Prophylaxis for Human Immunodeficiency Virus Infection after Sexual or Injection Drug Use Exposure: Identification and Characterization of the Source of Exposure," *Journal of Infectious Diseases* 184 (2001): 1608–1612.

24. R. Grant et al., "Preexposure Chemoprophylaxis for HIV Prevention in Men Who Have Sex with Men."

25. A. Karim and S.C. Baxter, "Antiretroviral Prophylaxis for the Prevention of HIV Infection: Future Implementation Challenges," *Future HIV Therapy* 3 (2009): 3–6.

26. Microbiocide Trials Network, "MTN-003 Phase 2B Safety and Effectiveness Study of Tenofovir 1% Gel, Tenofovir Disoproxil Fumarate Tablet and Emtricitabine/Tenofovir Disoproxil Fumarate Tablet for the Prevention of HIV Infection in Women," http://www.mtnstopshiv.org/node/70 (accessed October 6, 2010).

27. J. Levy, *HIV and the Pathogenesis of AIDS.*

28. Ibid.

29. P. Chigwedere et al., "Estimating the Lost Benefits of Antiretroviral Drug Use in South Africa," *Journal of Acquired Immune Deficiency Syndrome* 49 (2008): 410–415.

30. Avert, "HIV and AIDS in South Africa," http://www.avert.org/aidssouthafrica.htm (accessed November 14, 2010).

31. A. Dorenbaum, "Two-dose Intrapartum/ newborn Nevirapine and Standard Antiretroviral Therapy to Reduce Perinatal HIV Transmission: A Randomized Trial," *Journal of the American Medical Association* 288 (2002): 189–198.

32. J. Mrus, S. Goldie, M. Weinstein, and J. Tsevat, "The Cost-effectiveness of Elective Cesarean Delivery for HIV-infected Women with Detectable HIV RNA during Pregnancy," *AIDS* 14 (2000): 2543–2552.

33. J. Levy, J. *HIV and the Pathogenesis of AIDS.*

34. A. Coutsoudisa et al. for the South African Vitamin A Study Group, "Method of Feeding and Transmission of HIV-1 from Mothers to Children by 15 Months of Age: Prospective Cohort Study from Durban, South Africa," *AIDS* 15 (2001): 379–387.

35. C. Chantry et al., "Breast Milk Pasteurization: Appropriate Assays to Detect HIV Inactivation," *Infectious Diseases in Obstetrics and Gynecology* (2006): 95938.

Chapter 6

1. R. Shilts, *And the Band Played On. Politics, People, and the AIDS Epidemic.*

2. X. Wu et al., "Rational Design of Envelope Identifies Broadly Neutralizing Human Monoclonal Antibodies to HIV-1"; T. Zhou et al., "Structural Basis for Broad and Potent Neutralization of HIV-1 by Antibody VRCO1."

3. P. Johnson et al., "Inactivated Whole-virus Vaccine Derived from a Proviral DNA Clone of Simian Immunodeficiency Virus Induces High Levels of Neutralizing Antibodies and Confers Protection Against Heterologous Challenge," *Proceedings of the National Academy of Sciences, USA* 89 (1992): 2175–2179.

4. P. Guilfoile, "Two Case studies in the Scientific Method: HIV Vaccines and Antisense RNA Experiments," *American Biology Teacher* 61 (1999): 1–5.

5. B. Berkhout, K. Verhoef, J. van Wamel, and N.T. Back, "Genetic Instability of Live, Attenuated Human Immunodeficiency Virus Type 1 Vaccine Strains," *Journal of Virology* 73 (1999): 1138–1145.

6. J. Levy, *HIV and the Pathogenesis of AIDS.*

7. P. Berman et al., "Protection of Chimpanzees from Infection by HIV-1 after Vaccination with Recombinant

Glycoprotein p120 but not gp160," *Nature* 345 (1990): 622–625.

8. M. Girarda, S. Osmanovb, and M. Kieny, "A Review of Vaccine Research and Development: The Human Immunodeficiency Virus (HIV)," *Vaccine* 24 (2006): 4062–4081.

9. N. Flynn et al., "Placebo-controlled Phase 3 Trial of a Recombinant Glycoprotein 120 Vaccine to Prevent HIV-1 Infection," *Journal of Infectious Disease* 191 (2005): 654–65.

10. S. Rerks-Ngarm et al. for the MOPH–TAVEG Investigators, "Vaccination with ALVAC and AIDSVAX to Prevent HIV-1 Infection in Thailand," *New England Journal of Medicine* 361 (2009): 2209–2220.

11. HIV Vaccine Trials Network, "Step Study Follow-up Complete: First Analyses Presented at AIDS Vaccine 2010," http://www.hvtn.org/media/pr/stepfollowup.html (accessed November 14, 2010); R-P. Sekaly, "The Failed HIV Merck Vaccine Study: a Step Back or a Launching Point for Future Vaccine Development?" *Journal of Experimental Medicine* 205 (2008): 7–12.

12. S. Patterson, T. Papagatsias, and A. Benlahrech, "Use of Adenovirus in Vaccines for HIV," *Handbook of Experimental Pharmacology* 188 (2009): 275–293.

Chapter 7

1. J. Cohen, "Late for the Epidemic: HIV/AIDS in Europe"; J. Cohen, "HIV Moves in on Homeless Youth," *Science* 329 (2010): 170–171.

2. "UNITAID and the Clinton HIV/AIDS Initiative Announce New Price Reductions for Key Drugs," UNITAID, http://www.unitaid.eu/en/20090417198/News/UNITAID-and-the-Clinton-HIV/AIDS-Initiative-Announce-New-Price-Reductions-for-key-drugs.html (accessed November 14, 2010).

3. "Per Capita Health Expenditures by Country, 2007," InfoPlease.com, http://www.infoplease.com/ipa/A0934556.html (accessed November 14, 2010).

4. UNAIDS 2010, "Global Report: Treatment Coverage for Adults and Children, 2009," http://www.unaids.org/documents/20101123_globalreport_slides_chapter4_em.pdf (accessed December 4, 2010).

5. R. Smith, J. Li, R. Gordon, and J. Heffernan, "Can We Spend Our Way Out of the AIDS Epidemic? A World Halting AIDS Model," *BMC Public Health* 9 (2009): S15.

6. T. Hawkins, "Understanding and Managing the Adverse Effects of Antiretroviral Therapy," *Antiviral Research* 85 (2010): 201–209.

7. Ibid.

8. A. McCormick et al., "The Effect of Antiretroviral Therapy on Secondary Transmission of HIV Among Men Who Have Sex with Men," *Clinical Infectious Diseases* 44 (2207): 1115–1122.

9. P. Lamptey, J. Johnson, and M. Khan, "The Global Challenge of HIV and AIDS: Population Bulletin 61 (1)," Population Reference Bureau, 2006, http://www.prb.org/pdf06/61.1GlobalChallenge_HIVAIDS.pdf (accessed September 16, 2010).

10. R. Triboulet et al., "Suppression of MicroRNA-Silencing Pathway by HIV-1 During Virus Replication," *Science* 315 (2007): 1579–1582.

11. M. Tamhane and R. Akkina, "Stable Gene Transfer of CCR5 and CXCR4 siRNAs by Sleeping Beauty Transposon System to Confer HIV-1 Resistance," *AIDS Research and Therapy* 5 (2008): 16.

12. A. Kumar, "The Silent Defense: Micro-RNA Directed Defense against HIV-1 Replication," *Retrovirology* 4 (2207): 26.

13. B. Levine et al., "Gene Transfer in Humans Using a Conditionally Replicating Lentiviral Vector," *Proceedings of the National Academy of Sciences USA* 103 (2006): 17372–17377.

14. Ibid.

15. D. Richman et al., "The Challenge of Finding a Cure for HIV Infection," *Science* 323 (2009): 1304.

16. L. Naldini, "A Comeback for Gene Therapy," *Science* 326 (2009): 805–806; N. Cartier et al., "Hematopoietic Stem Cell Gene Therapy with a Lentiviral Vector in X-linked Adrenoleukodystrophy," *Science* 326 (2009): 818–823.

17. M. Tamhane and R. Akkina, "Stable Gene Transfer of CCR5 and CXCR4 siRNAs by Sleeping Beauty Transposon System to Confer HIV-1 Resistance."

18. G. Hütter et al., "Long-Term Control of HIV by CCR5 Delta32/Delta32 Stem-Cell Transplantation," *New England Journal of Medicine* 360 (2009): 692–698.

19. T. Mamo et al., "Emerging Nanotechnology Approaches for HIV/AIDS Treatment and Prevention," *Nanomedicine* 5 (2010): 269–285.

Glossary

adaptive immune response—An immune response directed at a specific pathogen. Normally this response requires one week or more to develop following infection. Antibodies, produced by B-cells, and cellular immunity directed by T-cells, are key components of the adaptive immune response.

adjuvants—Chemicals used to enhance the immune response to vaccination. Alum (aluminum oxide) is almost universally used, but others are being tested for safety and increased effectiveness.

AIDS—Acquired immunodeficiency syndrome, a disease caused by HIV, which is characterized by infections associated with a poorly functioning immune response.

antibodies—Proteins produced by a type of immune system cell called a B-cell. Antibodies bind to antigens, either on the surface of the microbe or to toxins or other molecules released by the microbes. The binding of antibodies to these antigens usually inhibits their function and enhances the ability of the body to destroy the pathogen or the molecules the pathogen secretes.

antigen—A molecule, frequently a protein, that induces the production of, and is bound by, antibodies. Typically pathogens, such as HIV, contain multiple antigens.

antigen presentation—An immune system process by which portions of a pathogen are presented on the surface of certain immune system cells. This presentation helps activate the immune response against that pathogen.

apoptosis—Programmed cell death. This is a natural "house cleaning" mechanism in the body for elimination of unneeded or damaged cells. HIV promotes unnatural apoptosis in immune cells in the body, contributing to the depressed immune response associated with AIDS.

autoimmune disorder—Disease caused by the immune system attacking the body's own cells and tissues. There is evidence that HIV may cause autoimmune disease in some infected people.

CCR5 antagonist—An anti-HIV drug that interferes with the virus binding to a key host cellular receptor, CCR5. Some strains of HIV are adapted to use this receptor, which is primarily found on macrophages, and the drug can help prevent virus entry into these cells.

CD4+ T-cells—A type of white blood cell that is one of the targets of HIV infection. CD4+ T-cells are depleted when HIV infection leads to AIDS. This severely damages the immune system because these cells coordinate both key arms of adaptive immunity.

CD8+ T-cells—A type of white blood cell that is usually important in controlling viral infections. CD8+ T-cells recognize infected cells and destroy them, thereby exposing the internal microbes to the immune system. These cells are sometimes called CTLs (cytotoxic T-lymphocytes).

centrifuge—A device for spinning liquid samples at high speed. A centrifuge separates, for example, blood cells from the liquid portion of the blood.

circumcision—A surgical technique in which the foreskin of the penis is removed. Several studies have demonstrated that circumcision can reduce the risk of transmission of HIV from both men to women and women to men.

complement—A group of proteins that constantly circulate in the bloodstream. In response to the appropriate signals that indicate an infection, these proteins become activated. As a result, the complement proteins are deposited on the surface of the pathogen, enhancing the ability of immune system cells to ingest the microbe. In the case of HIV, complement may have the adverse effect of enhancing the ability of the virus to infect some immune system cells.

condoms—A barrier method of birth control that can also reduce the risk of HIV transmission (and other sexually transmitted diseases, such as gonorrhea). A condom is a vinyl or latex tube that either fits over the penis, or is inserted into the vagina.

cytokine—A chemical messenger in the body. Cytokines act as a signal between cells in the immune system, which helps coordinate an immune response.

cytotoxic T-lymphocytes—A type of immune system cell that attacks and destroys human cells infected with viruses or bacteria (see CD8+ T-cells).

dendritic cells—A type of white blood cell that can be infected by HIV. Dendritic cells play an important role in communicating the presence of pathogens to other immune system cells. Their destruction by HIV compromises the immune response.

disability-adjusted life years (DALY)—A measure of reduced health and premature death as a result of a particular cause, such as AIDS.

DNA (deoxyribonucleic acid)—DNA is the genetic material of all organisms, and many viruses. It consists of four building blocks: adenine, cytosine, guanine, and thymine (A, C, G, T). HIV RNA is converted to DNA during the life cycle of the virus, allowing the virus to insert its genome into the genome of an infected cell.

DNA sequencing—A determination of the exact sequence of individual components of a DNA molecule (A, C, G, and T). This sequence can be used to identify genes, and to infer the genetic relationship between organisms.

drug resistance—The ability of a pathogen, such as HIV, to be unaffected by medicines that would otherwise prevent viral replication. Typically, drug resistance is the result of mutations that prevent the drug from interacting with specific viral proteins.

ELISA—A diagnostic test, usually used to determine if specific antibodies to a particular pathogen are present. In an ELISA, usually blood serum is taken from a patient and added to wells containing antigens. If the blood serum contains antibodies directed against the pathogen they will bind and can be detected. A positive test means that the person either has or had the disease, or at least had been exposed to the pathogen.

Env—The HIV envelope protein. It is made as a large protein, which is cleaved into two smaller proteins, gp120, and gp41. The gp120 protein is on the outer surface of the virus and is the receptor that docks with the surface of host cells to establish infection. The gp41 protein anchors gp120 to the surface of the virus.

enzyme—A protein that catalyzes a chemical reaction. HIV, for example, contains the enzyme reverse transcriptase.

fusion inhibitors—Anti-HIV drugs that prevent HIV from entering a host cell.

Gag—Group associated antigen, one of the key HIV proteins. Gag is a large protein, which is cleaved into smaller subunits, most of which play critical structural roles in constructing the virus.

genome—The genetic material of an organism or virus. Most genomes are DNA; for HIV and some other viruses their genomes are RNA.

genotypic resistance testing—A method for determining whether a person is infected with strains of HIV that are resistant to antiretroviral drugs. In genotypic resistance testing a section of the viral genome is analyzed for known sequence changes that cause drug resistance.

hemophilia—A genetic disease that causes uncontrolled bleeding due to a lack of a blood-clotting factor. Hemophiliacs are treated with infusions of blood clotting factors to prevent bleeding, and these clotting factors were often contaminated with HIV during the early 1980s. Consequently, in the United States approximately 50% of hemophiliacs were infected with HIV during the 1980s. Presently, a combination of heat treatment of clotting factors and the availability of genetically engineered clotting factors has reduced the risk of HIV transmission from this route to near zero.

highly active anti-retroviral theraphy (HAART)—The only effective treatment for AIDS; it involves multiple drugs, which attack different stages of the viral life cycle. For many people, HAART reduces the concentration of the virus to undetectable levels.

HIV—Human immunodeficiency virus, the pathogen that causes AIDS. There is a type called HIV-1, which causes the majority of infections in the world. Another virus, HIV-2, appears to be less pathogenic, but has caused some cases of AIDS, primarily in Africa.

IL-10—Interleukin-10, a cytokine that normally reduces immune function. Some HIV proteins induce the production of IL-10, which helps reduce the immune response against the virus.

immune system—The system in the body that fights infections.

infectious—Capable of being transmitted from one infected individual to another. An infectious disease is caused by a microbe that can be passed from an infected person to a susceptible person.

inflammation—A generalized, innate immune response to pathogens, injury, or other foreign material in the body. Inflammation is characterized by redness and swelling (resulting from increased blood flow) and the presence of cytokines and other chemicals in the blood that contribute to the inflammatory response. Chronic inflammation is one consequence of HIV infection and contributes to the pathology of AIDS.

innate immune response—An immune response directed against common molecules found on pathogens, but not specific for a particular pathogen. The innate immune response is available immediately after an infection. It consists of phagocytic cells, such as macrophages, complement, and a number of other factors.

integrase inhibitors—Anti-HIV drugs, which prevent a DNA copy of the viral genome from inserting into the host cell. The viral protein integrase is inactivated by these drugs.

Koch's postulates—A framework for identifying a particular microbe as the cause of the disease. Koch's postulates require that a microbe be isolated from an infected individual, that the purified microbe infect another individual, and then be isolated again from that second infected individual. Koch's postulates have been satisfied for HIV/AIDS through the accidental infection of laboratory workers with HIV isolated from patients who had AIDS.

long terminal repeats (LTRs)—The ends of the viral genome, consisting of identical sequences. The LTRs play important roles in the transcription of viral genes and the integration of the virus into the genome of the host cell.

luciferase—A light-producing enzyme found in some bacteria and fireflies. Luciferase is used in phenotypic assays for HIV resistance as a reporter for HIV replication in the presence of anti-HIV drugs. Higher light intensity means more resistant viruses.

macrophages—A type of white blood cell that can be infected by HIV. Macrophages typically engulf and destroy pathogens, and have the ability to rove around the body in search of microbes. When infected with HIV the mobility of macrophages can help distribute the virus throughout the body.

major histocompatability complex class I (MHC class I)—molecule on the surface of cells that presents antigens from intracellular pathogens. Also known as HLA (human lymphocyte antigen).

microbiocides—Chemicals that inhibit the entry of a pathogen into cells or otherwise prevent pathogen replication. Vaginal microbiocides may represent an important means of preventing HIV transmission.

microglial cells—Phagocytic cells in the central nervous system that normally act as a key part of the immune response in the brain and spinal cord. Infection of these cells with HIV probably contributes to dementia and other nervous system disorders.

mitochondria—Small organs (organelles) found in cells that produce energy and are critical for cell survival. The side effects from many anti-HIV drugs are thought to result from damage to mitochondria.

natural killer cells—A part of the innate immune response, natural killer cells can recognize infected cells and destroy them. However, pathogens like HIV frequently have evolved strategies that prevent infected cells from being recognized.

Nef (negative factor)—An HIV protein originally thought to down-regulate HIV replication but now known to have a variety of functions.

non-nucleoside reverse transcriptase inhibitor—Anti-HIV drugs that bind to a pocket on the HIV reverse transcriptase enzyme, and prevent the enzyme from functioning.

nucleocapsid—A protein-containing structure that surrounds the genetic material in HIV and other viruses. The nucleocapsid helps protect the viral RNA from being degraded.

nucleotide or nucleoside reverse transcriptase inhibitors—Anti-HIV drugs that mimic the natural substrates of reverse transcriptase and prevent the enzyme from making a functional copy of HIV DNA.

phagocytic cells—Cells of the immune system, including macrophages, dendritic cells, and neutrophils, which ingest and destroy foreign material in the body, including pathogens.

phenotypic resistance testing—A method for determining whether a person harbors drug-resistant strains of HIV. In this method, a portion of viral genomes from a patient are inserted into a modified HIV, and used to infect cells in culture. The infected cells are grown in the presence of a variety of anti-HIV drugs, and if the virus continues to grow, it is an indication that the person harbors drug-resistant strains of the virus.

Pneumocystis pneumonia (PCP)—One of the diseases of HIV-infected people that defines AIDS. PCP is caused by the fungus

Pneumocystis jiroveci (previously called *Pneumocystis carinii*). The organism is widespread in the environment, but typically does not cause disease in people with a normally functioning immune system.

polymerase chain reaction—A technique for amplifying a small section of DNA. This method is used for, among other things, detecting HIV in blood or tissues, to determine if the microbe is present. The reaction consists of DNA from the pathogen, DNA primers, DNA polymerase, nucleotides, and a buffer.

postexposure prophylaxis—A method of preventing HIV infection in a person exposed to HIV. Typically, the patient is given two or more anti-HIV drugs within one to two hours of a known exposure to the virus.

preexposure prophylaxis—A method of preventing HIV infection in a person at high risk of being exposed to HIV. The patient is given one or more anti-HIV drugs in anticipation of a potential exposure to HIV. This approach is being considered for individuals at high risk for contracting HIV, such as commercial sex workers.

protease—A type of enzyme that cuts proteins into smaller pieces. The HIV protease is critical for the ability of the virus to complete its life cycle.

protease inhibitors—Anti-HIV drugs that target the HIV protease, thereby interfering with the virus life cycle since the protease is required to produce several essential HIV proteins in their active form.

real-time (or quantitative) PCR—A diagnostic technique used to determine the quantity of HIV in the blood and other body fluids (*see* polymerase chain reaction).

retrovirus—A type of virus with a life cycle that includes a step where the viral RNA is converted to DNA. HIV is an example of a retrovirus.

Rev (regulator of virion)—An HIV protein that controls transcription of HIV genes.

RNA (ribonucleic acid)—The genetic material in some viruses, including HIV. RNA is made of four building blocks: adenine, guanine, cytosine, and uracil. The production of RNA is fairly error prone compared to the production of DNA, another type of genetic material. This is one factor that accounts for the high mutation rate of HIV.

SIV—Simian immunodeficiency virus, a pathogen related to HIV that infects a number of different species of monkeys in Africa.

Tat (transactivator of transcription)—An HIV protein that plays a critical role in regulating transcription of HIV genes.

vaccination—A method for preventing infection. Vaccination involves exposing a person to antigens from a pathogen, resulting in the development of an adaptive immune response. This immune response will then prevent infection if the person is subsequently exposed to the pathogen.

Vif (viral infectivity factor)—An HIV protein that enhances the ability of the virus to be transferred from cell to cell, and makes the virus more infectious. Vif may also play a role early in the life cycle of HIV.

virulence factors—Molecules, usually proteins, that enable a pathogen to grow and survive inside the body.

Vpr—An HIV protein that is important for viral replication.

Western blot—A test for determining whether antibodies in a sample bind to specific proteins. For example, in HIV diagnosis a Western blot is used to confirm whether a person has anti-HIV antibodies in his or her blood.

years of life lost (YLL)—A measure of how much premature death is caused by an infectious disease, such as HIV.

Further Resources

Books

Levy, J. *HIV and the Pathogenesis of AIDS*, 3d ed. Washington, D.C.: American Society for Microbiology Press, 2007.

Sax, P., C. Cohen, and D. Kuritzkes. *HIV Essentials*, 3d ed. Sudbury, Mass: Jones and Bartlett Publishers, 2010.

Web Sites

AEGIS: AIDS Education Global Information System
http://www.aegis.com

AVERT: Averting HIV and AIDS
http://www.avert.org

Centers for Disease Control and Prevention: HIV/AIDS
http://www.cdc.gov/hiv

Medline Plus: HIV/AIDS
http://www.nlm.nih.gov/medlineplus/aids.html

National Institutes of Health: AIDS/HIV
http://www.aidsinfo.nih.gov

U.S. Federal Government AIDS/HIV site
http://aids.gov

About the Author

Patrick Guilfoile earned his Ph.D. in bacteriology from the University of Wisconsin–Madison. He subsequently did postdoctoral research at the White-head Institute for Biomedical Research at the Massachusetts Institute of Technology. He is a professor of biology at Bemidji State University in northern Minnesota, where he has taught microbiology and medical microbiology, and is currently an associate vice president at the university. His most recent laboratory research focused on ticks and tick-borne bacterial diseases. He has authored or coauthored over 20 papers in scientific and biology education journals. He has also written five other books in this series (*Antibiotic-Resistant Bacteria, Tetanus, Diphtheria, Chicken Pox,* and *Pertussis*), a molecular biology laboratory manual, and a book on controlling ticks that transmit Lyme disease. He is particularly interested in conveying information about science to the public, and currently writes a monthly column on science-related topics for his local newspaper.

Hilary Babcock, M.D., M.P.H., is Assistant Professor of Medicine at Washington University School of Medicine and the Medical Director of Occupational Health for Barnes-Jewish Hospital and St. Louis Children's Hospital. She received her undergraduate degree from Brown University and her M.D. from the University of Texas Southwestern Medical Center at Dallas. After completing her residency, chief residency, and infectious disease fellowship at Barnes-Jewish Hospital, she joined the faculty of the Infectious Disease division. She completed an M.P.H. in public health from St. Louis University School of Public Health in 2006. She has lectured, taught, and written extensively about infectious diseases, their treatment, and their prevention. She is a member of numerous medical associations and is board certified in infectious disease. She lives in St. Louis, Missouri.